THE RUSSIANS

THE

RUSSIANS

LEONID VLADIMIROV

FREDERICK A. PRAEGER, *Publishers*

New York · Washington · London

FREDERICK A. PRAEGER, *Publishers*
111 Fourth Avenue, New York, N.Y. 10003, U.S.A.
5, Cromwell Place, London S.W.7, England

Published in the United States of America in 1968
by Frederick A. Praeger, Inc., Publishers

© 1968 by Frederick A. Praeger, Inc.

Library of Congress Catalog Card Number: 67–24678

Printed in the United States of America

CONTENTS

v

40527

THE RUSSIANS

1

 A PERSONAL NOTE,
BEFORE WE BEGIN

"What!" you may exclaim, "Another one of those books on Russia?" Yes, and then again, no. With rare exceptions, these books are written by the men and women of the West.

I am a man of the East.

I have been a foreman in an automobile factory, a tractor driver on a collective farm, a journalist in Moscow, an attentive listener at high conferences in the Kremlin, and a prisoner in one of Stalin's camps. I am grateful for most of these experiences. They have given me the knowledge and much of the insight that I have tried to put into this book.

There is an old saw about Russia that holds that, if you

are there a week, you can write a book about it; after a month, you can write an article; and at the end of a year, you are at last qualified to write a paragraph about that vast and complicated country. On this basis, perhaps, I am entitled to write many paragraphs about Russia, because I was born there, and I endured there, for forty-three years. Also, I am luckier than most people who write books about my homeland. Not only was I saturated in the personal experience of being a Russian, but my work took me to almost every corner of the country. I was able to meet a great variety of people, and I met them as one of themselves, a Russian.

It is quite impossible, however well you know it, to pack the largest country in the world into a book, and I have not tried. You will find few descriptions here, for instance, of the striking Russian landscape. After all, there are dense forests like the Siberian *taiga* in Canada, too. And there are also deserts in Africa. And there are deep rivers, picturesque mountains, and bustling, attractive cities in other parts of the world. Here, wherever possible, I have preferred to write about people. This book, then, does not claim to be comprehensive.

In these pages you will find facts and perceptions, stories and observations, and many of these are part of my own experience. Here, in London, I have sunk myself in books, magazines, and newspapers that are taboo in my own country. It is probable that my writing will occasionally reveal this vice.

In 1966, in the course of my first trip outside the Soviet Union, I was in Great Britain; and I asked for—and was granted—political asylum.

By that time, the life on which I was turning my back in Russia was one in which I enjoyed many advantages. I had an interesting and well-paid job as the head of a department in the editorial office of an important magazine. I lived in a small but private—and therefore prized—apartment in the center of Moscow. I was the author of books, from the proceeds of which I was able to indulge myself in that special luxury, a motor car. I was constantly traveling, even making trips to the countries of Eastern Europe. I spoke frequently on the radio, and appeared also on television. And I enjoyed the facilities of the best private fraternity in Moscow—the journalists' club. By almost any outward standard, I was doing exceedingly well. Life was good, for me. But was it?

Perhaps it was my father who started it all. He was a professor of mathematics in Leningrad, and he was my idol when I was young. I lived alone with him for the four years immediately before World War II because, after my parents were divorced, my mother remarried and moved off to Moscow. For those four years, especially, I looked at life through my father's eyes. That look, for me, was crucial.

They were frightful years, 1937 through 1940. A careless word could cost you your head. As did so many people in those times, my father faced every new morning with the expectation that it might be his last in his own home. He might be arrested during the day and hurried off to an official oblivion. He knew that rivers of blood were flowing through the country, drowning many and intimidating the rest. But he did not want his only son to become a total captive of the official tyranny. He staked out his area of rebellion in the forefront of my mind. He began to tell me quietly, in the evenings, the truth about what was going on in Russia.

He ran a great risk in doing this. It was not just that we could be overheard by the neighbors on the other side of the flimsy partition that divided our apartment. The risk was far greater than that, because, in those days, children often informed dutifully on their parents. The public atmosphere created by the "struggle against enemies of the people" was such that I could quite well have come to regard my own father as an "enemy." Especially since he was in fact an enemy—an enemy of the use of terror, of the suppression of freedom, and of the humiliation of the individual—of everything, in fact, that a good deal later came to be called Stalinism. His views were in direct conflict with those I absorbed regularly from my school, the street, the newspapers, the radio, and the cinema. All of these taught me that I was living in the happy, free world of rising socialism, illuminated by Stalin's genius, and that only a handful of wicked enemies were preventing the completion of a socialist society. For all that my father could guess, the morning after our first conversation might have seen me rushing off to the secret police, then known as the NKVD, and he was quite aware of that possibility.

But he did what he thought he must do. Step by step, he injected into my mind antidotes to the official versions of reality. I learned, among other things, that only a species of madness could have taken a doctrine that was based on human welfare and made human beings pay such an enormous price in blood and fear to bring it to reality.

My father passed away on January 29, 1942. He died of starvation, as many did, while Leningrad was under siege by the Germans. Some of his thoughts and feelings continued to live on in me. I survived only because, in 1940, I had left for Moscow to enter the Institute of Aviation.

Shortly after the war, when a fog of anti-Semitism began to spread across the country, I became somewhat careless. I got into the habit of asking people how they liked breathing the air of fascism. In those times, some people would—with caution—agree with me, while suggesting that I would be wise to hold my tongue. But I could not seem to follow this advice. In August, 1947, I expressed to a man I knew the opinion that the country was in the grip of anti-Semitism, and he informed on me. No one else had been present when I told him this, so the authorities had something of a minor problem. Unlike the savage prewar years, it was now necessary to have two witnesses before one could be subjected to a political arrest. The secret police addressed themselves to the requirements of my case, organized a fairly simple provocation, and in a short time I was arrested. The charge was "profiteering." After some prolonged judicial acrobatics, I was sentenced to seven years in prison. When Stalin died, in 1953, I was released from my imprisonment, along with many others. I shall not tell the story of my five and one-half years as a prisoner. Much has been written about that type of Russian experience, and mine was not very different from most. I would like instead to recall what I thought and felt when I was given my freedom in April, 1953.

The Soviet Union was then in a state of exhaustion and stupor, largely the result of Stalin's excesses. It was living only by the grace of inertia. But the stupor gradually passed, and more and more people began to understand—and to admit—that there was little in the Soviet Union that could be recognized as part of the dream of socialism. The politics of terror had just about played itself out, and drastic changes were now called for. I was able to hope now, with all the hope that my father's teachings had instilled in me, that at last things would begin to open up, would become better, and that the air would be worth breathing for a Soviet citizen.

The Twentieth Congress of the Communist Party of the Soviet Union (CPSU) in 1956 was the one at which Khrushchev denounced Stalin's many crimes. The primary purpose of the Congress was to dissociate the Soviet regime from the Stalin record. It was important to show that Stalinism was not a natural result of the one-party system existing in the country, but rather an unfortunate deviation from the Party line, produced by the evil genius of a single individual.

In my mind, hope continued.

In the next years, it became easier to talk about things. Today, the amount of open political discussion that takes place in Russia is far greater than at any time in perhaps forty years. During my own last years in Russia, whenever I gave voice to ideas that might be termed seditious, people would hear me out and then express their own ideas, which might be termed no less so. But the widespread discontent in the Soviet Union tends to focus on personal and local problems: the dreariness and the lack of creature comforts, the high cost of living, the lies in the newspapers. Almost to a man, even the malcontents believe that improvement is possible within the framework of the present system. The Revolution and Lenin are almost immune from criticism. Those who yearn for a better future in Russia expect no fundamental changes in the psychological prison that official constraints have made of Soviet life. There will be certain improvements in the decor, some new furniture perhaps, but that is about all.

Because I worked as a journalist, I was obliged in one way or another to serve the regime. But to spend the day working in the interests of the system, and then to spend the evenings declaiming against it behind the walls of my own apartment, was not something of which my father might have approved— if there had been an alternative. In time, an alternative presented itself in the form of a journey beyond the Soviet border, and I took it.

Far more than most people, I had been prepared for a break with my country—by my father and by my experiences in the prison camps, to give only two reasons. It is not easy to sever all links with the country you love, without the certainty that you will ever return there. Not every person is capable of taking such a life-wrenching step. This is one reason why most of the Russian writers, artists, and journalists who frequently travel abroad return to their Soviet homes. Another reason, of course, is that anyone whose loyalty is the slightest bit suspect is simply debarred from going abroad. In my own case, I needed several years of preparation to disarm the vigilance of the authorities. Not everyone who might feel as I did is capable of this kind of studious public self-containment.

Now, as I sit here in London writing these lines, I do not even have to ask myself if my efforts—and my choice—were worth the price. The air is freer here, and every breath affirms the good sense of what I did.

But still, always I think of my fellow Russians . . .

2

 HOW TO UNDERSTAND
A RUSSIAN:
SOME CLUES

There are many Russias, and there are many Russians. For
instance:

The first thing I do as I go out of the house in the Moscow morning is to sniff the cold air. I draw it in through my
nose, and if my nostrils freeze up, then I know the frost is
really hard. So, up goes the collar of my coat, and I step out
briskly. (I devised this procedure far back in my childhood
and long regarded it as a personal secret. Later in life, I discovered that my secret was shared by many others.)

I sniff the icy air and my nostrils freeze solidly at the very beginning of my breath. The Russian frost has its own particular color; there are bluish tints in the snow, while the air seems to be pink, with little flecks of ice sparkling in it. The frost also has its own sounds. The snow scrunches under your feet if it is not more than fifteen degrees below freezing. At twenty below, it makes a complaining squeak. Today it is even colder, and the snow is positively squealing underfoot.

The people going down the side street where I live keep themselves warm by walking vigorously, their eyes screwed up and their hands thrust deep in their pockets. A white, inviting vapor escapes from the doors of the shops, which are more crowded inside today than usual. This is because half the people who go in are not there to buy, but to thaw themselves out a little, to stamp their feet on the floor, and to wipe the tears from their eyes. Then off they go about their business.

That is Russia.

The sun is unrestrained and pitiless. It burns you up, it sets the body on fire, making it impossible to think of anything but the heat. "The sun of the steppe-lands is like a boiling kettle, pouring yellow boiling water over your back," wrote the poet Yuri Pankratov. In this quiet, cozy little town on the steppes, about half of the people are Kazakhs, and they have their own way of dealing with the sun.

It is almost unbearable to look at one of them during the hottest time of day. You will see a man walking in the heat wearing a long, heavy robe and a fur hat. Not a drop of perspiration shows on his bronzed face, and not much more than that of real expression, either. He looks alert but untroubled, in sharp contrast to those who are strange to the area, and who begin to suffer visibly when the thermometer rises menacingly.

The people here assure the visitor that there are two main rules for fighting off the scorching heat: Do not drink, and keep yourself well covered. They always observe these rules, and they never take an afternoon siesta, not even when the temperature is so high that an egg buried in the sand is hard-boiled in a minute. They just go on working their allotted seven hours a day, as they do in any other weather.

That, too, is Russia.

The white waste of the tundra of Chukotka. The landscape is vast, flat, and completely unmarred by any sign of animate nature—with one exception. Three of the local Chukchi, who stand outside the little log-built trading station with me, are discussing it—a sledge, still far off and barely visible, but drawing nearer. The men are trying to figure out who the man on the sledge may be. They know by heart not only the names, but every detail about the family life of everyone who lives within a radius of 300 miles. Before the sledge is close enough for its rider to be recognized, the Chukchi guess that it must be an old man by the name of Kheu. He will be needing a drink because he is to be married the next day. Ten minutes later, old man Kheu draws his dog team up gracefully at the door of the station. With a powerful movement, he thrusts deep into the snow the long pole with which he guides the team. According to the conversation I have overheard, he is 65, though to me he seems far older.

After an elaborate exchange of greetings, Kheu goes into the trading station for his drink. He appears to be unconcerned when he is told that there is no liquor on sale. With a friendly smile, he explains to the storekeeper that he simply *must* have a drink, because he is going to be married the next day. Once again the storekeeper replies that there is none to be had. Kheu, in the same friendly manner, again repeats his request. I am waiting to see who will be the first to lose his patience and burst out with an insult. But nothing like that

happens. Having convinced himself after yet another exchange that there really is no liquor to be had, the old man
looks around at the goods on the shelves. He points to something and says a few words. The storekeeper smiles.

"Of course. How much do you want?"

Kheu shows three fingers and is quickly handed three
bottles of Red Moscow perfume. For some reason, this perfume has been shipped across 6,000 miles of the Soviet
Union, from the capital itself. Kheu is a good and generous
bridegroom, I think, to be picking up three bottles of expensive perfume as a gift for his bride. But I turn out to be
wrong, or at least partially so.

All the perfume is not for the woman who will be his wife.
Standing there at the counter, Kheu takes one of the bottles
from its bright-red packing. Then he removes the cork and
solemnly drinks down the perfume. He coughs, pays his
eighteen rubles, picks up the other two bottles, and politely
takes his leave. As he departs, he exudes a faintly out-of-
character aroma.

— And that is Russia, too.

A brand-new Volga taxi speeds me along a narrow, well-
paved road southward from Novosibirsk. It covers the fourteen miles in fifteen minutes. Then, after a few twists and
turns, we emerge from the forest and come suddenly upon
an ultra-modern hotel—the "Golden Valley." Nine stories,
glass doors, every comfort. I have arrived at *Akademgorodok*
—the academy town—the scientific center in Western Siberia.
The first stone or, rather, the first beam of this town, which
now boasts some 40,000 inhabitants, was laid in 1955.

This is not my first visit. From the window of my well-
heated hotel room there is a fantastic view over the frozen
taiga. I can also see the very modern building that houses the
town's trading center. I reach for the telephone and call up
my friends. We agree to meet around half-past eleven at

night, the usual time to go visiting around here. At midnight, the room is filling up with wonderful people, the "neo-Siberians," as they call themselves. Both women and men are in sweaters, with loose-fitting, plain jackets. It is useless to try to guess who among these people is a postgraduate student at the university and who a corresponding member of the Soviet Academy of Science. Age is no indication, because the *Akademgorodok* is full of professors and even academicians who are under thirty. Many of them are important scholars, and each of them is a serious person, although humor is, of course, not absent from our talk. But our topic is not science. Instead, we talk about art, literature (especially poetry), music, and domestic politics. The party breaks up around five in the morning.

Once again, that is Russia.

In a poem that he wrote about ten years ago, Yevgeny Yevtushenko, the best known of Russia's younger poets, celebrated the national diversity with lines such as these:

> I am thus and not thus,
> I am industrious and lazy, determined
>   and shiftless,
> I am . . . shy and impudent, wicked and good;
>   in me is a mixture of everything from
>   the west to the east, from enthusiasm
>   to envy . . .

To paraphrase an earlier writer (in this instance a Roman): The Russian is human, and for that reason no virtue and no vice is alien to him.

The Weather and the Man

Modern Russia has always been ruled from the cities of the north, where it is not at all unusual to find bone-chilling temperatures of from thirty-five to forty degrees below zero in midwinter. And the winters in the north are usually long. Perhaps the harshness and gloom imposed by these fierce seasonal conditions enforce a spirit of toughness on all who live under them, a toughness necessary to survive. The need for iron authority expressed in direct and easily comprehensible doctrine goes out across the country. It is not only necessary, but is more appreciated that way. Russian poetry is filled with a special kind of melancholy that marks the human soul and that is expressed in continual references to the pervasive cold, snow, and wintry gloom. A country like France enjoys a temperate climate, and there one finds, if many are to be believed, a nation of individualists, each man in business philosophically, so to speak, for himself. But what if France was made to endure the Russian winter, the kind of prolonged siege of the spirit that turns most thoughts, most of the time, to the rude imperative of keeping relatively warm? In this sense, there are many parts of Russia that may give the impression of a huge lifeboat, in which the resolute passengers, toughened to their crisis, lean together out of necessity. They know that the bleakness of their natural condition imposes the need, perhaps temporary, to live under an iron authority.

The current leaders of the Russian state have somewhat relaxed this heavy grip on the thought and action of the Russian people. There are pressures to get them to relax this grip even more, but these pressures do not come from the so-called average man. This fellow is quite content with the main lines of the officially sponsored ground rules that govern his life. He is a conservative who stands solidly on the bedrock of the Communist system as it operates today. If he is a member of the large group that might be described as the urban lower class, or if he is a peasant, he is probably even more nationalistic about his country than are more thoughtful segments of the population. There is a tendency in the Russian personality, almost built-in through centuries of living under various types of autocratic rule, to submit only too readily to authority. As a rule, it does not occur to the average Russian, when he is informed of a new directive from on high, to think of arguments against it. By nature, he is likely to be uncritical and accepting. When the official line flashes a new signal, he moves uncomplainingly in the new direction.

Contrast this with what goes on in many countries of the West. When a new idea is set in motion there, whether in a classroom, an office, or a factory, areas of dissent become apparent as an almost natural reaction. When the new idea is one that is imposed by the government on the country as a whole, there is frequently a predictable response from sections of the community. Speeches are made, letters written to the press, and antagonistic opinion makes itself heard whenever two or more people come together. In all but the most oppressed countries, no official doctrine is permitted into public view without arousing at least a few murmurs of dissent, or at least coolness.

Only recently has the Russian tempered his tendency to accept readily every new ruling imposed upon him by the state. Voices are beginning to be raised, and even, on occasion, petitions signed and demonstrations held in protest. These outbursts, conventional in the West, are somewhat new to modern Russia, but they are becoming more frequent.

The Art of Lying Low

For half a century, the average Russian has been living under the influence of an official philosophy that has frowned on the idea of "the individual." It is the state, the group, or —to use a cherished Soviet term—"the collective" that is all-important. For this reason, the Russian is likely to be somewhat more inhibited than his Western counterpart when it comes to asserting himself. He sees himself as a member of the group. It is not easy for him to think that the group may be wrong and he may be right. This kind of attitude, so much a part of the imposed doctrine of Soviet life, is not ideally suited to produce leaders. All through the 1930's, when Stalin's purges and terrors were mowing down Russians by day and night, to hold a position of responsibility in almost any area was an invitation to disaster. For years on end, to be responsible was to be exposed, and to be exposed was, more often than not, to be sent off to the camps, to disappear without a trace. It is not surprising, then, that so many Russians prefer to be content with being a member of the team. The rewards of leadership and responsibility are obvious, but there is a backing away from them. Most people continue to follow the wise course—if that is what it is—of staying in one's place as a member of the group.

This tendency is most immediately noticeable in the way the people dress. If you were to walk down a street in Moscow, you would see a kind of lackluster sameness in the people's clothes. There would be few of the sparks of individuality of color and line and fashion that one commonly finds on the streets of a large city of the West. This, too, is a carry-over from the period when Stalin was boss. In those perilous days, to be different from other people in anything was to stand out, and to stand out was to call attention to oneself, and to do that was usually interpreted by the uneasy ruler as a threat to the proper administration of the Soviet state.

But one should not be misled into any easy assumptions about the monolithic nature of the Russian's basic character. The sameness of the clothes and the sameness of many of the actions are only a form of protective coloration—or noncoloration—to permit him to blend more easily into the surrounding landscape. He knows better than to call attention to himself. But in his heart, he is that same creature of fierce passions and uncontained emotions that figures so prominently in the great Russian literature of the last century. And he wears his heart much closer to the sleeve than do most Westerners.

The Russian Under the Skin

A Russian's feelings are close to the surface. When he feels something—if the feeling is not politically questionable—he thinks nothing of showing his emotion. Two men who are friends may meet on a street, and they will be so glad to see each other that they will kiss unhesitatingly, like French generals, but with more feeling. Subjected to such sudden emotional pressures as an excess of vast joy or anguish, the Russian does not dream of hiding his feelings. He lets go, and the air is filled with oceanic laughter or tears, cries of joy, or wails of sorrow. Breasts are beaten, bodies hugged, and the air shakes with the explosion of deeply felt emotion.

The man of the West—the Englishman, for instance—is the kind of fellow who usually appears to be self-conscious about his feelings and chooses to keep them out of sight when he is in public. The Russian is not self-conscious. His emotions are a basic part of him, and he finds no reason to make excuses for them or to hide them. He is a tough fellow who knows how to survive, barring the perversities of a dictator suffering from homicidal mania. He can adjust to any circumstances, the violence of winter or the debilitating heat of the worst summer. The most grievous shortages of the necessities of life will only make him pull in his belt, tighten his lips, and keep going. The Nazi siege of Leningrad, with its horrors, would have eventually felled many lesser men, but the Russian hung on, survived, and in time won out.

In his heart of hearts, there is a kind of wildness, a lack of restraint that borders on the anarchistic. It gives a tone of eccentricity to a part of Russian life, or at least to its history before the advent of the Bolshevik state imposed the higher wisdom of the group. This kind of grand eccentricity stems almost logically from the Russian capacity for giving instant expression to his feelings, whether of joy or violence, sadness or generosity.

All Russians understand this acting out of one's feelings. The outburst may serve at times as a safety valve, releasing pressures that, left to accumulate, might produce damage far more unpleasant to the individual or even to those around him. The community understands, and does not visit on the culprit the ultimate social horror, public shame and humiliation. He is viewed more tolerantly than he would be in most corners of the West. And as for himself, because he has violated the law or the code, he must pay the consequences. It does not occur to him to claim that he is being "framed," as the expression goes, or that there is something wrong with a society that finds it necessary to single out such as he for punishment. He accepts his penalty with calm.

He is inclined to be optimistic and even enthusiastic about most things, despite the many literary salutes to the notorious gloominess of the Russian soul. He has something else, too, which is a great source of strength to him. It is especially valuable in a world in which, now and then, events set off round-the-world repercussions that may shake the foundations of men's lives. The Russian has a sense of his own roots, of his own traditions, of belonging to a group, a community. This has great meaning for him. It provides an anchor of security when it becomes necessary for him to face the vexations earth and man are heir to.

In a way, the Stalin period returned the Russian people to that special relationship with their ruler that they have had throughout most of their history. For their occasional loaf of bread and the patch of roof over their heads, they were expected to offer total obedience, if not servility, to the will of the ruler who claimed to be their exclusive agent and representative.

Well, then, what have we learned about the average Russian? Not a great deal more, probably, than one may learn about the average American, or Englishman, or Frenchman.

He hungers for peace, but then so do most sane men. He is long-suffering and he is spontaneous, he has toughness and he has sentimentality. He is also very much interested in what goes on in the outside world and reaches instantly for any news of it he can get. It is unfortunate, of course, that so much of that news is carefully doctored by his authorities before he is permitted to absorb it. He has a great thirst for knowledge of almost any kind, and will read almost anything. It is not unusual for a book published in Russia in an edition of 100,000 copies to sell out in a few days. He works hard—his wife does, too—and he enjoys himself when he can. Because he loves the sight of green things, he soothes himself with plants if he lives in the city—they are in many windows. More than most other people, he is able to trust and believe in the essential goodness of human nature. Also, he is somewhat uneasy about the present, as who is not? And he looks forward to the time when things will be better, as who does not?

3

CITY LIFE:
ONE MAN'S ROUND

Joseph Stalin was not widely known as a dreamer, but he had his flights of fantasy. In 1936, for instance, speaking on behalf of the new Soviet constitution, he offered this notion:

> By force of habit the working class is often called the proletariat. But what is the proletariat? The proletariat is a class bereft of implements and means of production [belonging] to the capitalists [who] exploit the proletariat. . . . But in our country the capitalists have already been liquidated. . . . All possibility of the working class being exploited is precluded. . . . the proletariat of the U.S.S.R. has been transformed into

an entirely new class . . . emancipated from exploitation, the like of which the history of mankind has never known before.

It is more than three decades since the workers of the Soviet Union were informed by their leader of the ideal conditions under which they lived. To encourage the general belief in their good fortune, the official censorship has deprived most of them of any possibility of realistically comparing their working conditions with those in any major Western country.

There can be little doubt that the Russian suffers by such a comparison. In his own life, he may not be aware that he is worse off than, say, the worker in Sweden or America. But he is certainly aware that there are many things, many conditions under which he lives, that will in time have to be changed for the better, if the glorious aims of the Revolution are to be achieved. Or, to take a more down-to-earth approach, if life is to be made somewhat easier for him.

By the standards of the United States, the average Russian worker must keep extremely busy if he is to keep his head above water. In addition to his own immediate need for survival, there is the special feeling, imposed constantly upon him by the state, that he must do his share in making sure that the national aims are realized. His wife is unlikely to suffer from the problem that assails many American wives: What to do about her afternoons? As a rule, the Russian woman is doing with them exactly what her husband is doing —she is working through them. It is necessary for most Russian women to work, too, to help their family to stay afloat.

The average family will thus have two checks coming in with regularity. Among his blessings, the worker may count the fact that his rent is cheap, and will usually represent less than 4 per cent of his income. In many instances, the bills for such utilities as gas, electricity, and the telephone will not amount to more than an additional $15.00 per month.

Also, the state will educate his children free, and sometimes will send him and his family off on holiday very cheaply.

An Average Day

Try, for a moment, to put yourself in Russian shoes. You work as a mechanic in a tool plant in Moscow. You have been at your job long enough to know that you are better off today than you were, for instance, only ten years ago. But still there are aggravations, to say the least.

You get up in the morning in your apartment, the one you share with two other families. The apartment has three rooms, one of which is incontrovertibly yours. The sink, the toilet, the bathtub, and the kitchen, however, are just as incontrovertibly shared. It is around six o'clock, and your wife begins to make breakfast. If you have ever seen a Western magazine of the glossier kind, it may occur to you that your wife looks a bit older for her age than foreign women seem to. This is because she has had to work so hard. Despite all that hard work, however, she is likely to be somewhat heavier than a woman of her years in the West. But this thought is unlikely to occur to you.

At seven o'clock, you and your wife leave for your jobs. Your son goes off to school. Now that the five-day week has been instituted, you will work a bit longer during the day than you did under the former five-and-a-half-day regime. But you are not so unwise as to think that you will be coming home immediately after your official stint is concluded. Very frequently, you will get home late, because large amounts of your own free time are expected to be offered by you for different services to the state. There is work to be done at the plant to meet quotas, and you have "volunteered" to stay to do it. There are meetings you must attend, perhaps to help in the arrangements for the celebration of the next political holiday. And there are other unavoidable demands on your time. But even with all this, you are aware that it is easier for you to breathe these days—things are not as bad as they were under Stalin.

You have eaten your lunch at the factory canteen, but now you are ready for home and a nice hot meal prepared by your wife. When you arrive at your apartment, the kitchen is jammed with people, but you are used to this. You have been sharing this apartment with those other two families for some time, now. They, too, must make their supper, and you long ago learned to steel yourself to the conventional Soviet kitchen smells of other people's cabbage, tobacco smoke, and newly washed clothes. You dream a little now, perhaps, about all the new housing units that seem to be springing up, and you hope that someday soon, somehow, you will be able to move into one of these with your wife and child. It would be wonderful, you may think, to come home at the end of a working day to an apartment with several rooms that are all your own, and to which no other family has a key.

Practically everyone you know is full of complaints about the problem of privacy, and talks of how nice it will be when there are enough of those new apartments to go around. At the moment, however, there is just not enough space for everyone. There is, in fact, a legal minimum of space permitted each tenant, and this is fixed at eight square meters; but, as with so many rules, this one, too, is violated. You may have less. If you do, then you will think oftener of the apartment you have applied for in that new building. You will think of the waiting list, too, on which you might possibly remain for seven or eight years, or more.

Consumer goods are becoming more generally available, and you and your friends, when possible, are accumulating such items as television sets, refrigerators, and transistor radios. This has caused concern to some citizens who adhere to the old-line Party sanctions against private property. But you do not share this anxiety, because your newspaper has come out with severe editorial reprimands against those who have expressed such concern. Private property is bad only when it is a symbol of capitalistic excess. But it is right and proper for those living in a Leninist state to have personal possessions. You and those whose opinions you hear most frequently are all anxious to accumulate whatever personal possessions and other signs of well-being that you can manage.

One thing you would really like to see is a greater general availability of decent clothes. All about you, men and women are dressed in humdrum fashion, in clothes designed for use, rather than for appeal to the eye. You have heard stories about men who offered to buy the coat or shirt or tie right off the body of some Western tourist in Moscow. You know that such things are frowned upon by the authorities. You have probably heard, far too often, the joke about Adam and Eve:

What nationality were they?
Russian.
Why Russian?
Because they didn't have any clothes, had only an apple to eat, and were told that they were in Paradise.

The problem of food is an old one, of course, and you are probably used to it. When there is a queue outside some store, you can be sure, most of the time, that the people have lined up to buy something edible. And you know, for instance, if you happen to like fresh vegetables, that you might as well forget about them in the wintertime. They are just about unprocurable then.

Some years ago, Eugene Varga, one of the leading economists in the Soviet Union, was asked a question that might have been embarrassing. Why, he was asked, was there such a continuing shortage of goods in Russia, while a capitalist country like the United States seemed to have a somewhat different problem—an excess of production in most areas? The answer, according to Varga, was "because the income of the working masses in the capitalist countries is not sufficient to absorb the volume of goods with which the capitalists constantly flood the market in pursuit of profit." To most Western experts, this was a brilliant—and hilarious—misconception of the case. But you would probably not be aware of that.

Your taxes, at least those you are aware of, are quite low, but you are paying extra to the government in the form of more money for food and consumer goods. The government usually raises the prices of such items. This serves the double function of bringing it additional money and acting as a form of rationing.

Should you get sick, you do not have to worry about medical bills. The state will see that you are taken care of. Your doctor is likely to be a woman, because three out of four Soviet doctors are, but this does not concern you in any way. Nor will you be aware that the doctor does not enjoy the relatively eminent status that is the doctor's reward in a country like the United States. A doctor in Russia is just another citizen trying to do his—or her—job. There is no charge, either, for any dental work you may require. Here, if you are like most Russians, it will not occur to you to be perturbed by the lack of concession that Soviet dentistry makes to your vanity. Chances are you will be unaware that, by Western standards, your false teeth will seem almost ostentatious, while fillings in your front teeth may be quite noticeable.

Despite television and the general loosening of the strictures that tied you down for so many of the earlier Communist years, you may be getting more restive under the constraints of your limited social life. There is not enough novelty or variety in it. This may not actually be a bother to you, yet. But you know a number of people by now who are, to use a common Western term, "bored." It is not just that your newspaper contains no comic strips or gossip columns. It is perhaps that the old puritan ideal of Soviet man as a "working animal" has not yet been made to give enough ground.

The Cost of "Just Living"

You will probably be getting your wages paid to you at the end of every two-week period. Like most of the people with whom you have personal contact, you will spend the next two weeks trying to juggle those wages to gain the maximum benefit for your family and yourself. Here, in American terms, are some of the prevailing prices:

1 pound of bread	$ .08–$ .14
1 pound of cheese	$1.60
1 dozen eggs	$1.50
1 pound of sugar	$ .50
1 pound of meat	$1.00–$1.30
1 pound of apples	$ .40
1 pint of milk	$ .20
1 pound of ham	$1.95
1 pound of butter	$1.85

This last item provides the opportunity to recount a Russian joke which is so old, and still so widely heard, as to constitute almost a part of the national heritage:

A boy, in the year A.D. 2000, has been reading something in a book and has a question about it. He turns to his grandfather. "What is a queue?" he asks. The grandfather explains how, in the old days, butter used to be in short supply, and people would have to line up for it. The boy then asks, "What's butter?"

There are times when you will have to buy things besides food. A sampling of the prices for some of these items is as follows:

Man's ready-made suit, poor quality	$ 90.00
Man's winter overcoat, poor quality	$110.00
Same overcoat, reasonable quality	$250.00–$300.00
Pair of leather shoes, cheapest quality	$ 18.00
Poplin shirt	$ 7.00–$ 11.00
Pair of women's stockings	$ 3.00–$ 4.00
Small-screen television set	$187.00

Women's dresses, furniture, crockery, and many of the other essentials of everyday life are quite expensive by any standards. For example, a Czech folding bed (a very important item of furniture in one-room Soviet life) costs about $260.

It should be obvious from prices such as these that you, as an average urban worker, would have to be an everyday economist of near-genius to make your way through the year-round ordeal of the wages and prices gantlet. Sour types have been known to point out that, in view of the frequent shortages of items in special demand, the Soviet worker is lucky. He has only to think of the prices of these items, and to contemplate the money he is able to save when he is not able to purchase them. The average wage for a good factory hand is about $23.00 a week. A foreman gets $25.00, and some engineers get $28.00. My wage, as head of an editorial department of a popular magazine, was $49.00 a week. By the same yardstick, it is perhaps just as well that there is a distinct shortage in Russia of restaurants and cafeterias, of laundries and dry-cleaning plants, of barbershops and shoe-repair shops. These are always quite crowded. Those with especially lean purses can feel grateful that they are spared here, too, the need to spend their money.

In your own case, for winter wear you have bought a light coat of rather poor quality. It is the best you can afford. Your wife has probably made it considerably warmer for you by sewing a padded lining into it. This kind of coat is known as a "seven-season model," because it is likely to be worn until it drops off the owner's back. The process of altering, mending, and otherwise attending to necessary repairs in one's wardrobe is something that keeps the women of Russia busy during the average evening. For this reason, you, as a worker, will probably wear your oldest clothes to your job.

It is not easy to improve your lot. In most countries of the West, it is at least possible for the working man to move to some other area to find a better job opportunity. But this is not possible for you in the Soviet Union, where a system of internal passports is in force. In about three dozen major cities, you will be denied the automatic right to enter and reside. You must first produce proof that you are needed by some specific local employer, and that he has guaranteed to provide housing for you.

A few years ago, a group of Soviet economists worked out the minimum wage on which a single Soviet citizen could subsist. It was based on the most modest needs: the minimal quantity of calories necessary to maintain normal health; one suit of clothes a year; one overcoat every three years; a visit to the cinema once a week; a cheap seat in the theater every two months, and so forth. It developed in this study that the average person required the equivalent of $89.00 per month, given the Soviet price structure and the array of government benefits. Anything less than that was judged to be manifest poverty. As a worker in that Moscow factory, you would be making perhaps half that amount of money each month per each member of your family, but you would not be aware that, officially, you were considered to be below the line of marginal living. The results of the study were never published. What *was* published was the promise that at the end of the next projected five-year plan, the real wages of Soviet employees would increase by 20 per cent. This notably happy event is officially scheduled to take place by 1970.

More statistics. They are all about you in your life. They explain something here, offer a more or less convincing excuse there, rouse you to dreaming—to enthusiasm, perhaps—elsewhere. Now they lure you on, now they hold you back. It is hard to guess at such things, but it is possible you might miss statistics if they were abolished from the Soviet scene. They are like an old friend who is somewhat disreputable, but you have become used to him. You do not mind so much that he is something of a liar now and then. You have become used to that, too.

4

 FITTING THE MIND
FOR ITS UNIFORM

"Wherever is found what is called a paternal government, there is found state education. It has been discovered that the best way to ensure implicit obedience is to commence tyranny in the nursery." This statement was made in 1874 by Benjamin Disraeli. It bears a family relationship to an old Russian proverb that says you should train a child while he can still lie across the bed; once he requires the whole bed to lie down on, it is too late to teach him anything. In the Soviet Union, the system of education is based on the wisdom of this proverb.

Children make up a specially favored class of the Soviet

state, not because the leaders suffer any special excess of sentimentality over thoughts of infant darlings, but for reasons far more practical. The youngest generation represents the Russia of the future. Few efforts are spared to ensure that that Russia will conform to the blueprint that its present leaders have designed for it. Most nations tend to shape their educational processes to those ends which will best serve their own needs, and these needs are not always merely political, economic, or religious. The Soviet Union pursues this policy of shaping the young mind with a particular directness and even relentlessness. And it begins early.

The overwhelming majority of Russian women work on an equal footing with their husbands. A woman who is pregnant is given paid leave in her eighth month, and this pay continues until two months after her child is born. If the mother chooses to extend her leave to a year, she may do so, but at her own expense. Few women are affluent enough to take advantage of such a luxury, and most, therefore, get back to work at the end of the period of paid leave. As a result, millions of infants are handed over to nursery schools. These institutions, which look after children from the age of two months to three years, are widely distributed around the country. A mother will breast-feed her child in the morning and then take it to a nursery school in the vicinity of her factory or office. Four hours later, she has the right to take an hour from work to go off and feed her child. Those who have plenty of milk may leave some of it in a bottle at the nursery for their children. At the end of their working day the women or their husbands collect the children and have them at home until the next morning. When the period of breast-feeding is over, the situation becomes easier, and the mother no longer has to visit the nursery in the course of her working day.

From the second year of their lives, the children in the nursery school are taught to speak, and in some places also to sing and dance. Special teachers play games with them that are the thoughtful creations of the preschool training sector of the Soviet Academy of Pedagogics. By the time the child has reached the age of three and "graduates" from the nursery, he is already somewhat literate, politically. He will know a number of engaging stories about "Uncle Lenin, who was the nicest man in the whole world." In another time, he would have heard such stories about "Uncle Stalin." He will have learned that "in the old days our country used to be ruled by a wicked czar, but then the workers and peasants overthrew him and started to rule the country themselves"; that "the best and cleverest people in our country join the Communist Party and are called Communists"; and even that "across the ocean, in America, live the wicked bourgeois people, who want to kill all the Communists and put the czar back in his former place." By the time he is three, the child also knows about the invincible Soviet Army and the glorious frontier troops who guard the country by night and by day, never letting the enemy cross the borders.

From the earliest possible age, Russian children are taught not only to love, but also to hate. Wicked enemies, crafty bourgeois capitalists, lie about in the world, waiting to spring upon the unwary. These creatures occupy the place in many Soviet children's stories that are occupied in other national literatures by dragons and bogey men. Should you, as a parent, attempt to teach the child something different in the evenings, the collision of your authority with that of the teacher may produce psychological problems for the child. He may very well turn away from you. That is one reason why, even among mothers and fathers who may be troubled by such curiosities of Soviet indoctrination, there is usually little effort to mitigate with their own reason or experience the heavy doses of propaganda pressed upon the children.

From the ages of three to seven, the young Soviet citizen may attend the next educational institution, the kindergarten. The cost of sending a child to one of these is not high, averaging about $10.00 per month, including meals.

In the four years he spends in a kindergarten, the child acquires a great deal of information. Some of this knowledge, however, is likely to be of the sort that can only produce disquiet. Often enough, the child may come to notice the discrepancy between the stories about happy childhood in the Soviet Union, part of his regular schoolroom diet, and his own life with his family at home. He becomes aware of the inequality between people, even between the children in his kindergarten. For the first year or so he may ask parents and teachers the most baffling questions. One of my four-year-old son's classmates once asked him in a matter-of-fact way, "Say, Mitya, when your father comes home drunk, does he beat your mother or not?" Mitya replied that his father never came home drunk, with the result that he was himself immediately beaten for telling an obvious lie. "What do you mean, your father never comes home drunk? Everybody's father comes home drunk!"

Teachers in kindergartens are very experienced women who are not easily surprised by their pupils. They know how to give the ideologically correct answer to any wild question on social, religious, or political issues. If they notice that a child is going too far with such questioning, they will warn the parents to keep away from dangerous conversational ground in front of him. Sensible parents do as they are told.

One result of this process is that the young boy or girl gradually acquires what is an extremely important faculty in Soviet society. He develops an understanding of which questions one can ask or discuss, and which ones must be avoided. When he is an adult, this special prudence can be useful. As a grown-up, should he play a role "on the ideological front," perhaps as a Party official or as a journalist, he will be considered to have good political sense, which is no mean commendation. On less obviously exposed fronts, this faculty of political self-preservation will help him through his life with a minimum of unpleasantness. It is wise for the employee to know when to keep quiet, when to shout "Hurrah!" and when to lean forward, ever so carefully, to offer "constructive criticism." This kind of criticism is encouraged, within certain limits, in the Soviet Union.

In the kindergarten, the staff makes a tremendous effort to instill into the children the sense of "collectivism." In practice, this means the unquestioning submission of the minority to the majority, and of everybody to the one leader. "They are all eating their porridge, but you are not—shame on you!" "They are all singing the song about the red flag, except you. Are you against all the others?" The greatest offense a child can commit in a kindergarten is to be different. Children are very anxious to be "like the others." If, one morning, a mother wants to dress her boy in something new which seems to him rather too noticeable, he may refuse, saying, "They will tease me about it." The children acquire a special "collective zeal," so that they pick on any signs of individuality in their schoolmates and do their best to suppress them. The "individualist" is likely to be ridiculed, or even set upon by his fellows, and they may complain about him to the teacher. This eagerness for expressing the superior merit in the values of "all right-thinking people" goes beyond what is to be found in most societies. Few nations make it easy for the individual who wants to swim against the current of prevailing mores, but the Soviet Union makes it almost impossible.

From ages seven to fourteen, all Soviet children are educated at school. Coming together into these schools are two separate streams of children, those who have been attending kindergarten, and those who have been educated at home. The former are in the majority, and are likely to dominate most classroom activities. But primary-school teachers are quick to admit that the children who have been educated at home until the age of seven are as a rule more interesting—more intellectual, better mannered, and even more affectionate.

The teacher who makes this judgment, however, is likely to prefer working with the children who have already been through kindergarten. They provide fewer individual problems and are far easier to deal with. The child from the kindergarten is less capricious, less demanding, and less sensitive than the one who has been educated at home. He is inclined to unawareness of himself as an individual, and sees himself more as a member of a group. He is accustomed to taking minor difficulties without complaint, and he probably knows by now that the concept of "justice" is somewhat relative. And he also knows that it is important for him to be careful about when to speak up.

The Group Is Always Right

It is the main concern of the teacher to "make a collective of the class," as the process is described in Soviet manuals. Children from the kindergarten make it easy to accomplish this, while the children who have been educated at home will only get in the way. It is not the teacher's wish to discriminate against any student, but an atmosphere of discrimination is nevertheless brought about. This is because any show of individuality cuts across the teacher's aim. Also, the children from the kindergarten are always in the majority, and they invariably make the others fall in line. If they sometimes do this with a child's cruelty, the teacher accepts that cruelty as an unavoidable evil. He is, after all, himself a product and a supporter of the "collective" idea. He was brought up in the same way and will never oppose the majority. And if the mother of a "home-educated" child comes to him with a complaint that her child has been beaten or teased, that he cries bitterly at home and does not want to go to school in the mornings, the teacher knows what to say: "You know, your son is not used to the collective. He's a bit of an individualist. The sooner he gets this out of his system, the better. The rest of them are good children, and he'll make friends with them in the end. But he finds it difficult to start with, and they find *him* difficult too. That's why they don't get along at the moment. But don't you worry— I'll see that they don't maltreat him, and you, on your part, try to get it into his head that it's not right to complain about the collective and that he must adapt himself to it." The mother sighs like a parent, but gives in like a citizen. With the passage of time, the child does indeed stop complaining about the school and adjusts himself by one means or another. He either acquires the qualities of a "full-fledged member of the collective," or he retreats into himself and sooner or later is left in peace.

Meanwhile, the process of political education continues uninterrupted. Of the eighty pages of the book of the Russian alphabet—a picture book used in the first year—sixty-three are devoted either to Lenin or to the Revolution, the Party, the Kremlin, the Soviet Army, or similar topics. The book contains short stories, pictures, and poems, which the children have to learn by heart.

The school year begins on September 1, and the teacher begins almost immediately to prepare the children for the national holiday on November 7, the anniversary of the Revolution. Each child is given a poem or a song to learn and perform at a special meeting to be held in the school. Even before they are able to read, the young people learn to recite aloud these poems and songs of propaganda. Their parents usually help by reading the poems to them at home. It is unlikely that any parent, even the rare one who may be somewhat depressed by the uninspiring content of such material, is going to refuse such help to the child. For one thing, the child might mention the refusal to the teacher. This could cause considerable trouble. For another thing, the child would be deeply offended. He would not be able to understand why every other pupil's mother and father were helping to prepare him for the celebration, while his own refused.

With certain gradual changes in the method, this kind of teaching continues for a minimum of seven years, and in most cases for ten. More and more children in the Soviet Union are now receiving not the seven-year but the so-called full secondary, or ten-year, education. In the course of his schooling, the child inevitably becomes a member of political organizations. At the age of eight he is admitted to the ranks of the "Octobrists." At ten, with even more ceremony, he enters the Pioneers, and on that occasion, he makes the so-called solemn promise. This is a sort of oath of loyalty to the Party, taken in the presence of his schoolmates.

At the age of fourteen, the school child has the chance to enter the Komsomol, the Union of Communist Youth. This is an important organization. While he is at school, it will dominate student activities. It will also provide a great deal of weight in determining who will go on to university. For an applicant to get into a university, there must be some evidence that he is politically reliable, and membership in the Komsomol provides him with a built-in security clearance. It is, in its way, a kind of equivalent to what serves in some Western circles as a "loyalty oath." Membership in this organization is considered to be voluntary, although there is, as can be easily imagined, a great deal of pressure to "belong."

Still, a large number of Russian students hold back. The average student seems to find somewhat more interest in his books and studies. He is more interested, too, in giving his spare time to hobbies and sports, and, where it is possible for him, romance. The line of demarcation between those who join and those who do not has become more obvious in recent years. Despite this, the number of students who sign up for the Komsomol represents approximately half the total to whom this official blessing is offered.

Russian students are encouraged to attack their studies by cramming, and they leap to the learning process with a special joy. The love of knowledge is everywhere evident, and it is not hard for the authorities to adjust this love to the needs of the Party line. Whenever possible, the student is made aware of the way in which the class struggle affects people in this world.

The Soviet Union grinds out more graduates in the fields of science, agriculture, and engineering, in proportion to the population, than does any other country. It is not surprising, with such practical emphases in education, that the humanities get short shrift in the halls of learning. Facts are continually popping out at the student, some of them dignified as "fact" only out of the special tolerance provided by political considerations.

Those who have chosen to join the Octobrists, the Pioneers, and the Komsomol have to pursue an additional subject in their organizations, one that might be called "hierarchism." In all these children's political organizations there are chosen leaders to whom the others must defer. They are selected in accordance with the procedure of Party democracy. That is to say, they are elected by vote, but the ones elected always turn out to be the ones who were "recommended from above." In this way, some acquire the beginnings of careerism, others learn yet again to submit without questioning, and everybody comes naturally to the idea of having a hierarchy. The idea of collectivism—the subordination of the minority to the majority—the idea of hierarchism—the subordination of the majority to a tiny minority—do not come into conflict in most minds.

Politics Everywhere

A Russian's political processing is by no means over when he finishes school. It continues throughout his conscious life. To start with, there is the fact that people regularly read newspapers and magazines, go to the theater and the cinema, listen to the radio, and watch television. Stalin's view that "the press is the sharpest and most effective weapon in the hands of our Party" has lost none of its force. The press, radio, cinema, television, and a certain type of literature continue daily to fill the heads of grown-ups with variations on the conventional themes to which the children had been originally tuned in when they were at the nursery.

Wherever a man may work, he is always under the supervision of the local Party organization. Even if he is not a member of the Party, he must be "educated." That word, which is used to describe the process, has an almost official status, and even if the pupil happens to be past fifty and to enjoy the title of professor, he must expect that he will be "educated." Study circles and seminars are organized everywhere for the consideration, mainly, of the history of the Soviet Communist Party or of Marxist philosophy. The "Party educational network," as these circles and seminars are called, operates every year from October to June, like an adult-education institution spread across the entire country. In every office, workshop, scientific laboratory, restaurant, cinema studio, taxi garage, collective farm—in short, everywhere—one day a week is called political-instruction day. On that day, people stay behind after work for an hour, or maybe two, to absorb the wisdom of the Party under the direction of its propagandists.

Few people actually enjoy this political training. Should there arise the slightest opportunity to miss a lesson, the average student is likely to seize it without hesitation. This is true even of members of the Party. But few people make the mistake of flatly refusing to take part in these instructive situations. The Party has a handy label to attach to any such dissenters: "Refused political instruction." It is a dangerous label to carry around, when it is glued to one's career. The Party organization will see to it that this rare person will not be promoted, will not be awarded any bonuses, and won't receive permits to holiday homes. And, of course, his chances of traveling abroad, even to Eastern Europe, are gone forever. Only a lunatic would want to get himself into such a state of functional disgrace. What would be the point? It is far easier to sit quietly through one's hour or two on political-instruction day, doodling on a bit of paper, and hearing for the hundredth time about Lenin's struggle with the Mensheviks.

The authorities consider, however, that even regular political instruction is not an entirely satisfactory means of "education." So, apart from that, there are national programs for the "study of current Party documents." Thus, for example, three months before the fiftieth anniversary of the October Revolution, the Central Committee's department of propaganda published an enormous yawn-inducing document of some 25,000 words. This was the so-called Theses of the Central Committee of the CPSU concerning the Fiftieth Anniversary of October. For three months running, those theses were "studied." That is, they were read aloud in all offices and similar group contexts.

Throughout this period, the newspapers would announce with appropriate solemnity such newsworthy insights as the following: "The steelworkers of the Magnitogorsk metallurgical plant are studying enthusiastically the historic programmatic document. . . ." Or, "The cowmen of the Red Ray collective farm have begun their study of the Party theses in a state of great elation. . . ." And so it goes. Propaganda perseveres throughout the life of the individual. It is a major industry and a major social force.

But when all is said, it must be admitted that the Soviet attitude toward learning has brought distinct benefits—along with everything else—to the average citizen. At the time of the Bolshevik Revolution, three people out of every four in Russia were illiterate. In Siberia, the ratio of illiteracy was probably even higher. Today, it is hard, although possible, to find an illiterate in the Soviet Union.

For the child who is being educated in that country, the future stretches out ahead rose-filled, sunny, bright with promise. It is only later, as he moves along the process of education and personal growth, that he may become aware of a certain distance between the earlier promise and the later fulfillment. He looks about him and notices that the norms of his original dream have never been fulfilled. It is only natural that then, since he is human, there may be evoked in him a tremor of distress. This reaction, so much more customary in areas bathed in "bourgeois sentimentality," is likely to induce in many Russians the memory of one's youth. That, after all, was the time of joyful beginnings, when every goal seemed possible if only one reached for it. It is interesting to note, by the way, that when official authority permitted the publication in the Soviet Union of J. D. Salinger's "Catcher In The Rye," that very romantic celebration of youthful disillusion with an adult world, it became an immediate best seller.

The Hope of the Future

"The youth is our future, our hope, Comrades," Stalin said in 1933, and in a way that might not have pleased him, he was right. The young people he was talking about in that faraway time are today running Russia, but they are doing it with considerably less rigidity and with far more relaxation of the state's controls than Stalin himself usually considered necessary to a well-run country. Those who are beginning to come of age today, more than a generation later, may, in time, give an even more liberalizing turn to Stalin's hopes.

As with the arts, the youth of any country may serve as a barometer of any oncoming heavy weather in the society. The young people of the Soviet Union, at least the youth in the major cities, are currently in a state of unrest, if not agitation. Their fevers derive from many pressures, but the important thing is that the fevers exist and that they are made plain. For example, this deeply romantic cry in a letter to the press:

> I earned good money and lived alone, far from my parents. I worried about them no longer because I had been working since I was seventeen. I set out to find a world where I could enjoy "cheap caresses." There were friends, parties in the evening, with cards and playing with "the old bottle." . . . within our four walls it was another world. Here we read the verses of A. V. Koltsov and Sergei Yesenin, of Alexander Blok and Yevgeny Yevtushenko, clarifying the essence of life in the tobacco smoke. Here the "twist" was beat out boldly, and the cynical proclamation was made, "I love life . . . I love it big . . . like a woman lying before me . . . and I'll . . . have her!" I left my job, lost my registration in town, and went "underground."

This kind of hymn to bohemia might be heard in almost any country and in almost any time, but what is surprising is that this one was sung recently in the Soviet Union. Its like had not been heard in the workers' fatherland for some forty years, and even then, in those bold carousing days of the 1920's, the smell of the successful Revolution still warm in the nostrils of the young, those who sang it usually managed to tie the theme in, somehow, with the new Soviet state.

Other letters reveal other signs that all is not at rest in the young Soviet heart. A certain Vasily N. expounds the philosophy that you should "live yourself and let others live." Apparently this means, among other things, that although he likes his wife, he is ready to turn her in for any other attractive woman who comes within reach. And "there are stunning ones!," he assures the reader.

A young physicist writes that he loves his work, but he seems to love love almost as much. For him, love is a serial form of entertainment. He seeks affairs, shying away from the woman who demands the deepest attachment. In his view, the whole idea of the family is only a form of old-fashioned prejudice. Fortunately, he believes, in its present aspect it seems to be dying out.

In 1960, the Soviet youth newspaper, *Komsomolskaya Pravda,* founded its own variant of the American Gallup Poll. This was a team of journalists that carried out a poll, presumably on the hypothesis that if enough of them asked questions of enough ordinary citizens, they would occasionally get honest answers. In a poll conducted in 1961, it was discovered that many young people in Russia have a "bourgeois" point of view and suffer from a pronounced you-only-live-once concept of reality. Many girls, apparently, spend their time mooning over the prospect of a rich husband, while large numbers of boys, suffering less obviously from the disease of capitalist thinking, are dreaming of beautiful wives. By official standards, both activities are counterproductive. Additional violence was done to Soviet objectives by the discovery that far too many young people drink, and spend their energies in dancing and in the admiration of foreign movies. One girl was quoted as complaining that any life dominated by Komsomol activities was bound to be dull, yielding only "meetings, dues, and paper forms."

In Moscow, there is a group of young people who have banded together under the name of "The Society of Young Geniuses," and their manifesto proclaims that "Every person passes through a period when he is in conflict with the life of his society, with his world, and with himself. It is our duty to reflect this conflict, this anguish, and these thoughts." These are noble words and, of course, unthinkable in the Soviet Union of the past generation. This, too, is a sign of the surge of new energies among at least a segment of Soviet youth.

It is only natural that the official press has poked fun at these young people—when it has not sought to chasten them more grimly. For instance, the initial letters of the Society

of Young Geniuses, in Russian, spell out SMOG, and journalistic imagination has leaped to the possibilities. But even
Komsomolskaya Pravda, special mother hen of Soviet youth,
while waxing stern on this youthful effusion, was driven to
note that it was a protest of the young against the shallowness
and lack of honesty in much that is official in Russian life
today.

To most alert persons of the West, this rumbling from
down below is expressed most obviously in the marginal type
known as the *stilyagi.* In this group is the fellow who expresses his revolt against society by wearing sharply tapered
pants and showing a pronounced preference for American
jazz and movie stars, foreign cars, and, if he can lay his hands
on them, dark glasses. Many of them are likely to be the sons
of families in the higher reaches of Soviet society, while
others are the less responsible offspring of the urban poor.

The *stilyagi* are especially interesting as a social symptom.
Under the rule of "collectivism," by which children are
trained, it requires considerable courage or lunacy to go
against the direction of the group. Russians tend for this
reason, among others, to be among the most conservative
people in the world, where the proprieties—and the way one
dresses—are concerned. When the first *stilyagi* made their appearance, perhaps a dozen years ago,* they produced a sense
bordering on outrage among their more conventional fellows.
Groups of young Communists prowled the streets in those
days, hunting down young people who dared to show themselves in tight pants, fancy shirts, or dark glasses. In such
holiday resorts as Sochi and Yalta, on the Black Sea, the
police were arresting and fining men who went around in
shorts and women who wore dresses that were excessively
low-cut. I remember an official of the Young Communist

* The words *stilyaga* (singular) and *stilyagi* (plural) were first used by a
certain Belyaev, a humorist, in a story published in *Krokodil* magazine as
early as 1953.

organization in Zaporozhe, in the Ukraine, telling me with enthusiasm about the special attention given to these rebels in his own area: "Our patrols catch those narrow-trousered types, drag them into the nearest doorway, and cut off one trouser leg with a pair of scissors. Believe me, it has a wonderful effect!"

Today, narrow trousers have become almost accepted wear. This is true also of shirts worn outside the trousers. The struggle of the present to hold back the future continues, however, in the matter of long hair for young men and short skirts for young women. But even there, the status quo is giving ground. These pernicious Western influences, too, will be generally accepted, in time. Then the battle lines will shift into some new area in which the future has begun to assert itself.

Under the old conventions of official constraint, in the time of Stalin, for instance, it was easy for the press to label the rare expression of youthful nihilism as some kind of psychotic aberration. After all, since the Russians were living in the best of all possible worlds, there could be no objective reason why anyone but a crazy man—or perhaps a "capitalist dupe"—could find any need to rebel against it. In the somewhat freer air of today's Russia, it becomes harder to use that argument, especially since this kind of rebellion is no longer the infrequent individual expression of the past.

Throughout his education, the young Russian has been trained to accept the word of his leaders as being ultimate wisdom. Any tendency to doubt, to question, or to express skepticism has been crushed. Despite the systematic attempt to nurture only the most "official" responses in the individual, something very human, something quite individual, in fact, has remained uninstructed and uncrushed in large numbers of Russia's youth. Among those who feel most deeply, the need to doubt and question—and to express that doubt and that questioning—is beginning to show itself more openly. The result, in the prevailing atmosphere of continuing official displeasure, is a kind of spiritual unrest.

Today, it is largely among the youth, and most particularly in their poetry, that one finds the kind of hope implying the possibility of change. That change would have as a basic tenet the loosening of the corset that has constrained the spirit of the Russian people. What many young Russians begin to yearn for is a better chance to realize their equity in that universal dream—to make something truly worth-while of one's life.

5

 IN THE FACTORY

I shall never forget the day, in the summer of 1955, when I was first introduced to my job in the engine workshop of the Moskvich small-car factory, in Moscow. Two years earlier, I had been released from a prison camp. Now, after finishing a course at the Institute of Auto Mechanics, I was to be a factory foreman.

Another foreman, in blue overalls, was showing me around the workshop on that first day. As I walked down a narrow, dirty passage between two rows of lathes with this unsmiling fellow, he would stop every few paces to explain something to me. His words could barely be heard through lips that

scarcely opened, and it was difficult for me to follow everything he said. His factory jargon and Tatar accent made matters no easier for me.

In the course of the tour, he would sometimes take me up
close to one of the lathes, to point out a detail. If there was a
worker standing at the machine, and if he was in the foreman's way, he would be shoved casually to one side. There
would be no attempt to introduce me to him as the new
foreman. Often enough, my guide would not even bother to
look at the man he had just pushed out of the way. Apparently, this did not surprise anyone. The worker would
move obediently to one side and wait in silence, watching us
out of the corner of his eye, until the bosses were through.
The third time this happened, when my guide treated an
elderly woman worker in this way, I said to her, "Good day.
Please excuse us." The woman muttered a brief "It's all
right," while the foreman seemed not to have paid the
slightest attention to our exchange. From then on I greeted
each worker as we came to him. Some acknowledged the
greeting and others did not.

When the trip around the factory was over, and we
emerged from the labyrinth that was soon to be my responsibility, the foreman offered me a few final words of advice.
Most of what he had to say was connected with technical matters, but he ended in a rather unexpected manner. "And now,
about the work people," he said in his cool, unemotional
voice, "There are in this section thirty-seven machine-tenders
and two tool-setters, both of them Communists. They're not
a bad lot on the whole, but you don't want to try any of your
'Excuse me, how do you do?' business with them. There are
no educated people here, and they don't understand that
kind of approach. They'll get the idea that you're too easy,
and before you know where you are, they'll be on top of you.
Then you'll only have yourself to blame."

I should like to describe that factory, where I worked as a

foreman, technologist, and one of the editors of the plant newspaper. About 14,000 workers were employed there in producing the Moskvich small car, and the factory is considered to be one of the best in the country. It is shown with considerable official eagerness to foreigners, and there are very few in the Soviet Union that are revealed in this way. Even today, I can recall every corner of that great plant, because although I left it, in time, to become a professional journalist, I never lost contact with the people who worked there. They used to discuss things quite openly with me, and even invited me into their homes at the workers' housing estate not far away.

Just inside the gates is an avenue that runs right into the middle of the factory. Here, everything is clean, the pathways are lined with trees, and there are carefully kept lawns. This main roadway is sometimes called the Avenue of Honor, because to the right and to the left of it there are large portraits of the factory's "leading people," primarily employees who have exceeded their quota of work.

But the most impressive part of the factory is the main assembly line. Here, as with the rest of the plant, all the equipment—the machines, installations, and even the tools—were transported from Germany at the end of World War II. They were used there in producing the automobile known as the Opel "Kadett." The working drawings of that automobile were appropriated as well, so that the Moskvich-400, which went into production in 1946, was an exact copy of the earlier German car. The later model could be distinguished from the original only by the badge on its front end. This car went on being produced in the U.S.S.R. until the middle of 1956.

It would appear to be axiomatic in some Western countries that the manufacturer of a major consumer product like an automobile constructs it in such a way that the car will become useless in a relatively short time. It will then have to be replaced with one of the newer, shinier models. As a result, the new infusion of the consumer's money into the economy will increase the manufacturer's profits and perhaps even make a contribution toward keeping the national economy on a reassuring keel.

There is no such "built-in obsolescence" deliberately incorporated into the manufactured products of the Soviet Union. But for a variety of reasons, including shortages of materials, bureaucratic ineptitude, and occasional lack of know-how, the same result may be achieved by accident, rather than by design. For six long years, for example, large numbers of Moskvich-402 cars mercilessly ate up their front tires with undue rapidity, because it was impossible for the engineers to figure out a way to adjust the front wheels properly. Some of these cars were turning their tires "bald" after running for only 500 miles, a situation that might turn a privately operated motor company to thoughts of bankruptcy.

The result in Russia was somewhat different. The production of tires for the Moskvich had been planned with no thought of the voracious appetite of its faulty front suspension. In addition, the factory did not dare to report to the government that it was producing poorly designed cars and therefore needed an increase in the output of tires. As a result, prices for the tires shot up to fantastic levels in the regular shops (about $50.00 each). On the black market, as might be expected, the price was three times as high. But even at such prices, few spare tires were available.

It was not until after about six years of this that the Moskvich engineers, with the help of experts called in from the Gorky automobile plant, managed to correct the engineering fault.

Because the bureaucracy frequently ignores existing shortages, refusing to revise its expected quotas downward in the face of reality, there is a kind of joke, often along these lines:

"Did you hear about the hen that committed suicide on the collective farm? It left a note that said 'I'm ending it all. I can live without love, but I can't live without a system. They don't give me any corn, but they still expect me to give them eggs.' "

Russians have long been accustomed to persist in the face of a wide variety of unpleasant conditions. In many workers, there is a remarkable quality that enables them to wriggle out of the most difficult situations and to somehow make something out of nothing. Official propaganda refers to this quality often, using the phrase "Russian wit" to describe it. It is better described, perhaps, by the old saw "Necessity is the mother of invention."

This national talent is exploited on a large scale. Leaders at various levels have acquired the habit of telling their underlings "It *has* to be done." When an employee hears those words from someone in authority, he knows the order must be carried out at any cost and at the expense of whatever superhuman effort it demands. Because, having given the order, the man in authority has shifted all responsibility for the job on to the subordinate. If anything goes wrong, the latter will not get out of it by talking about "objective causes." Bosses in Russia don't bother to listen to explanations.

In the Moskvich plant, for example, stoppages occurred quite often, sometimes more than once in the course of a single shift. A frequent cause was the shortage of component parts, which were supposed to be delivered by other factories. We had a heavily staffed "department of cooperation," which was responsible for "extracting" supplies from other factories and from even less obvious sources. To be the man in charge of this particular department is the most unnerving job in any plant. However hard he may try to keep his supply lines in order, some shortage of supplies is bound to develop, and no explanation or excuse for this failure to provide is acceptable. It becomes his fault.

Such jobs are important in any production hierarchy, but the turnover in them is great. The men who hold them may be dismissed in disgrace with a reduction in rank and a Party reprimand. If they can hold off disaster for a time, they will try to arrange more or less smoothly to have themselves transferred to positions less obviously exposed on the production front. At Moskvich, in my time, this department was run by Semyon Kitain, a man of iron nerves who had formerly been an officer in the State Security Service. "I've got a first-class job," he used to say to me bitterly. "At any minute I'm liable to lose my Party card or have a heart attack."

How Industry Pays

Wages in most Soviet factories are paid on the piecework system, and at first sight this appears to be quite reasonable—the more you do the more you get. Unfortunately, the system rarely works out equitably.

On my first day as a foreman at the Moskvich plant, I was approached by a tool-setter in my section.

"Comrade foreman," he said somewhat hesitantly, "the men have to be moved around on their jobs. Will you do it—or would you rather that I did it until you get used to the job?"

"Where do they have to be moved from—and where to?"

The tool-setter smiled at my ignorance and proceeded to enlighten me. It turned out that there are great differences between the piecework rates paid for doing various jobs. There are poorly paid operations on which a worker receives something like twelve kopeks for turning out 100 pieces; and there are well-paid ones, at which he might get as much as 200 kopeks (two rubles) for 100 pieces. In theory, these jobs differ in the amount of skill and time they demand, but in practice there is hardly any difference at all. It is simply that some operations pay the worker well and some pay badly. To keep the assembly line moving, each section must, naturally, carry out all the operations without any exceptions. So my problem was how to make a worker perform functions that were, in contrast to others, unprofitable for him. Under such conditions, the only way to keep everyone happy was to switch the jobs around fairly regularly, and this, subsequently, took up the greater part of my time.

Thus, the earnings of a machine operator under this system of "piecework" payment depend not on his qualifications nor on how hard he works, but on the decisions taken by the foreman of his section. If you are on good terms with the foreman, he will see that you get well-paid jobs, and your wage-packet will get bigger. If your relations with the foreman are cool, you may just have to tighten your belt. And as a rule, it will do you little good to complain.

I know of many cases in which workmen who thought they were being treated unjustly in such situations went over the head of the foreman to complain to the workshop trade union committee. But I don't recall a single case in which any satisfaction was provided. A committee representative would arrive at the section and he would proceed to examine the job sheets. Officially, there was nothing to justify any legitimate complaint, he would point out. The petitioner might protest that he was being kept at a low-paid job, while others were enjoying the largesse of being shifted around. There would be no real hope for him. The reply from above is predictable: "Your complaint is unfounded. The work you are doing is in accord with the rates laid down. There is no breach of the labor law here. If you want to keep your job here, then get on with it. If you don't, then clear out."

It is only natural, then, that every workman's first concern is to get on the best possible terms with his foreman. I was quite surprised when, on the first payday after I came to the factory, two of the men in my section invited me to supper with them and produced a bottle of vodka to go with the meal. Bowing to tradition, they were extending a little hospitality to the new foreman at some expense to themselves. The moment the invitation was offered and the bottle shown, however, I understood what was happening. I turned the men down with some difficulty, because it was hard to convince them that I would be able to keep on good terms with them without letting them provide me with such graces.

There are foremen, of course, who do not refuse such invitations, and this is only one way to improve relations with one's immediate superior. There are others, of which the most infallible is quite straightforward: bribery with money. The men may take up a collection among themselves and give it to the foreman, along with a list of the contributors. Once this is done, the foreman is able to allocate the available jobs in a way that is calculated to satisfy everyone. Everyone on the list, in any case. This system is particularly widespread in garages and taxi organizations, where the drivers pay a regular fee to those in charge, to get more congenial assignments.

Too much consideration on the part of a foreman can, however, be dangerous. For example, I had in my section an absolutely first-class machine operator, named Ivan. He was not only highly qualified, but an extremely hard worker. He had a very large family, and for this reason tried to increase his wage by forcing as much work out of himself as possible. The tool-setters told me privately that I could give Ivan every opportunity to earn more money, that the other workmen knew about his special difficulties and would not take offense.

At the time, I lacked experience in such matters and went a little too far in my efforts to help Ivan. For a whole month, I gave him only well-paid work, with the result that at the end of the pay period he was due to receive a sum that by ordinary standards, was astronomical. The day before the men were to receive their wages, I was called to the labor and wages department at the main office. There I was given an angry dressing down. "What do you think you're doing, paying people amounts like that?" I was asked. I explained that Ivan had earned his money honestly. For my pains I was called a "naïve infant," and was told in great detail how important it was for me, as a foreman, to control wages in my section. The payment of a machine operator must never rise above a particular figure, I was told, or it would be considered excessive. When there *was* such an excessive payment, it was further explained, the factory might be accused of deliberately reducing its labor quotas, of concealing the possibility of raising the productivity of its labor force, and other sins.

"If you're really concerned about your work people," said the head of the department toward the end of the conversation, "then you won't allow any more cases like this to happen. Otherwise, they will raise our quotas and reduce the rates accordingly. Then your people will get nothing for their work. Do you get me? So there you are. Now I'll just knock thirty rubles off the pay of your record-breaker, and you just explain to him what I've done. Unless he's a fool, he'll understand."

Ivan understood.

The Tyranny of the "Norm"

Every six months, each Soviet factory reviews its "norms." The operation can be extremely painful for those who are subjected to this official probing, because, according to Communist theory, all plants must be constantly raising the productivity of their labor. According to the same theory, productivity is expected to rise at a faster rate than the workers' wages. To permit reality to adjust itself to the dialectical needs of this official theory, output quotas may have to be raised as often as twice each year, with a corresponding reduction in the rates of pay. Thus, the productivity of labor can be seen to increase in relation to the prevailing wage bill.

To accomplish this semi-annual miracle, an army of economists and labor experts descends on the factories, along with accountants and bookkeepers, to shake up the work quotas, squeezing at the performance levels as opportunity shows itself. In their wake, new norms are left to be fulfilled. The director of the factory never makes the mistake of protesting at the fresh exorbitant demands being made on his men and machines. He knows that his is not to reason why.

"Shame-Sheets" and Other Incentives

If you were to visit a Soviet factory, your attention might be drawn to a large notice-board near the entrance, which seems to bear some rather dramatic information. Translated, it may say something like this:

> **FLASH!**
> The fitters' brigade, led by Komsomol Yuri Novozhilov, in the course of the pre-election competition, turned out nine cars more than their quota in one shift. Congratulations!
> **TO THE LEADERS!**

Workers are continually being exhorted to outdo themselves in honor of specific occasions that may be counted on to bring out the heroic in the average citizen. Such noteworthy opportunities abound in the average working year. To boost production rates, appropriate posters are plainly visible to acknowledge publicly the virtues of the diligent. They are also around to call attention to those who have proved unworthy of the effort expected of them. For instance, alongside that first poster there might be one like this:

> **SHAME**
> on the manager of the blacksmith shop, Starostin, and the foreman of the hot-pressing section, Vinogradov. Because of their failure to deliver hub castings, the assembly of the front suspension in the chassis shop was brought to a halt.

In addition to the public humiliation thrust upon them by the "shame-sheet," these men will not get any bonus for the month.

Another kind of poster, less immediately personal, may simply cry out

ATTENTION! ATTENTION!
Today at 1530, there will be a PRE-ELECTION MEETING in the factory yard. Agenda—to propose candidates for election as deputies to the SUPREME SOVIET of the U.S.S.R.
EVERYBODY TO THE MEETING!

This kind of poster is likely to be put up only five minutes before the end of the shift. As an additional precaution to guarantee maximum attendance, the factory guards will have been instructed not to let anyone out of the gates before the end of the meeting. If the workers had known of such a meeting sufficiently in advance, many of them might have become suddenly "sick" and, armed with a note from the foreman, gone off to the medical room and eventually to the meeting-free sanctuary of their homes.

"Private" Industry

How can the monthly plan be carried out if workers must stand idle for many hours because of shortages or the breakdown of old and worn-out machines? There is only one way, and that is to put in an extra two or three hours at the end of their regular shifts. But this is not called overtime. Foremen are warned not to put in for overtime payments for their men, regardless of the circumstances. The men may be paid only the normal piece-rate that prevails on their regular shift. It is the foreman's job to persuade, as best he can, the men in his group to bend themselves to these after-hour needs. That is why he has been made a foreman.

I soon came to understand what was required of me in these cases. In effect, I had to be especially ingenious at swindling people. Perhaps I was lucky that the piece-rate system offers vast scope for this kind of facility. For example: Our section had, among its other duties, the responsibility for assembling water pumps, and the rate of pay for this was very low. Even the most skillful and hard-working fitter could not make much money at it. My two tool-setters and I made it a practice to help the man assigned to assembling these devices, devoting every spare minute to speeding the process. In this way, a sizable sum of money was accumulated, in addition to what was earned by the fitter for his own efforts. By manipulating my own records with prudence, I was able to allot portions of this money to any worker I chose, simply by noting that he had performed some suitably appropriate function for which the money should be forthcoming.

As a result of this little deception—there were others—whenever the month's plan had to be pushed, I could go to the men in my section and say, "Look here, my friend. You'll have to stay behind for a few hours today, and turn me out a couple of hundred cylinder heads. There'll be a five-ruble bill for your trouble."

The worker would invariably agree.

Hidden funds, created by such a deception as the one noted here, serve as the grease that smoothes the production line in many Soviet factories. Such funds are also used to pay for many of the services not provided for by the piecework system. There is, for instance, no provision in any production chart for the job of transporting the various parts about the factory. In a piecework context, who is to be assigned to this time-consuming labor, for which no pay has been allocated? Here, the hidden funds can persuade a worker away from his regular assignment, at least temporarily.

Trying to pick up money over and above one's normal earnings is something of a national hobby in the Soviet Union. And there are many people who are able to wriggle their way around regulations with considerable profit.

Then and Now

The leaders of Russia have long been aware that the methods of production, the quality of what is produced, and the wages system could do with improvement. Premier Kosygin and Nikolai Baibakov, chairman of the State Planning Commission, have been particularly concerned with these problems. They know the special obstacles in the path of real improvement. It is the past that has cast a shadow over the working conditions of the present.

Briefly, it boils down to the following: In the period of Stalin's industrialization of the country in the 1930's, there were two powerful forces helping to advance the growth of Soviet industry—enthusiasm and fear. The first was generated by those men who had taken part in the Revolution of 1917. Many were genuine idealists who regarded the Revolution as their own work, and were ready to endure all kinds of privations to make Russia a paradise for their descendants. They were a selfless, ascetic people, and regarded concern for personal well-being as "bourgeois degeneracy" and a betrayal of the interests of the Revolution. At the time, their influence on the young was very great; young people set a high value on individual heroism, and "the old men," as they were called, really were exceptionally heroic.

Enthusiasm for work was further aroused by the shrill cries of the press and radio. The young Komsomols of the 1930's worked like demons in the factories and on the construction sites. And they lived, often enough, under harrowing conditions, starving, and even dying, with revolutionary slogans on their lips.

After a while, enthusiasm came to be replaced by fear. Stalin set about the destruction of the "old men" who had fought for the ideal of revolutionary equality. The police apparatus began to grow noticeably larger and more terrible, demanding and swallowing fresh victims at an alarming rate.

An epidemic of informing broke out, in which son informed on father, and brother on brother. By the middle of the 1930's, a prison-camp empire had taken shape, with millions of people behind barbed wire, that was a built-in slave state.

What could the average worker outside the barbed wire do in such a situation? He could not open his mouth to protest against any acts of injustice. To do so might earn for him the label of "enemy of the people." He could not betray the slightest slackening of enthusiasm or diligence at work, or he might be accused of sabotage. He was afraid not to shout "Hurrah!" when it was expected of him, because many people had disappeared into the camps, he knew, merely for keeping their mouths shut.

Life was unpleasant, to say the least, for the men who ran industry then. At any moment they could be arrested for a reason that had no noticeable relationship to logic or reality. But as long as such a man remained in his position of power as, for instance, the director of a factory, the actual business of keeping things humming was relatively simple. Work was based almost entirely on compulsion and fear. When the whip was cracked, the workers leaped to meet their quotas. There was no concern for the ordinary realities of factory management.

Today, fifty years after the Revolution and thirty-five years after the rule of compulsion and fear began, the old enthusiasm is just about gone. Fortunately, the fear is largely gone, too. Few workers today take very seriously the newspaper appeals to get one's back to the wheel, or the rosy pictures of the future. And people are also less frightened of the secret police. The economic factor has become the decisive one.

The attention of the top leaders is now concentrated on the economy. They no longer use empty phrases about "socialist competition" or talk of the imminent arrival of Communism, as even Khrushchev still liked to do. They are trying to improve matters in industry by economic measures. The economic reforms introduced into production, announced in the autumn of 1965, are directed by Kosygin and Baibakov. The essence of what they are trying to do is fairly simple: They want as many as possible of the people engaged in production, right down to the ordinary workers, to have a direct interest in making the work of the enterprises profitable, and therefore productive. To do this, they are taking their cue from the ideas of Yevsei Liberman, professor of economics at Kharkov State University.

According to Liberman (or according to the decisions of the Party, as you wish) industrial enterprises are now to pay for the basic resources—buildings, installations, and machinery—that have hitherto been theirs without charge. They must also have an interest in the marketing of their products, and they are now encouraged to conclude contracts directly with the buyers. Factory directors are being given the right to decide for themselves the size of their own labor force and technical staff. Also, they can vary these quotas in accordance with the demands of production. If, as a result of good work, the factory makes a profit, part of it may be distributed among management and the factory and office workers, in the form of bonuses or additional pay. Finally, the factory directors are given a limited right to change the wages system and, in some cases, to abolish piecework.

I once asked a friend of mine, an engineer-economist who had been given the job of converting the Moskvich plant to the new economic system, what he thought of the reforms. "Well," he said, "I think things will become easier for our factory. Especially if we can throw out the piecework system, get rid of a couple of thousand idlers from the factory, and offer some real incentives to those workers who are really productive. I have already put these proposals down on paper and the director has supported them, but will they give us permission to carry them through? That's the question."

"Why is that the question?"

"Because the reforms have already been introduced in hundreds of factories, and the results have not been too good. Most of them started by cutting down the number of people on the payroll. Under the new system, you still mustn't overspend on the total wages fund, even if it promises to bring in a substantial return in the future. And the directors were delighted to have the possibility of dividing the pie among a smaller number of people."

"So what happened?"

"We all know what happened—unemployment. For fifty years we haven't had it, and now here it is. But you aren't allowed to talk about it in public. We have no unemployment exchanges, no unemployment pay, and our personnel people are running around with long faces, because they don't know how to refuse work to a man who shows up and begs for it."

The new system was tried on a pilot basis with several clothing factories, and then extended into other areas. Bureaucrats with a stake in the old way of doing things threw up roadblocks on occasion, but the program continued. Being far from the Soviet Union, I cannot claim to have an insider's view of what is happening at the present time, but as far as one can tell from the few facts officially released, the new mode of planning continues to spread. Looming in the Soviet economy, perhaps, is a more obvious relationship between production and the needs of the consumer. And perhaps a new relationship, too, with that graceless capitalist entity, "profits."

6

 THE LIFE
OF THE HEART

Here is a letter that appeared in *Komsomolskaya Pravda* not very long ago:

> I'm only twenty-two years old . . . . I know by now how people say one thing and do another. I've seen those who use words to denounce depravity but then turn around and plunge into it with their lives. I've seen girls—"bargains"—who pose as "touch-me-nots," but in words only. I've got into the habit of seeing in them only a means of amusement. . . . There's only love for money, for a gay life. . . . I know you won't publish my letter, because it would be a black mark for your educational work.

This letter, from one who signed himself "Leonid," provoked many letters in response. A young man about his own age confided that "those who live only for others and not for themselves, actually are haters of life." The writer, taking pride in his selfishness, announced plans to live exclusively for himself. He went on to express only a limited enthusiasm for work: "According to the program for the development of Communism, all the work will eventually be done by machines. What is expected of me is enough, and when I have completed that, I stop." He suggested that in these times almost everyone he knows is a philistine.

Nikolai Ladnov is a man who would probably never dream of taking his troubles to a newspaper. Several years ago, he came to national attention when it was revealed in a criminal case that he had been applying to his love life an essential principle of Communism: from each according to his ability, to each according to his need. This was "no old-fashioned Don Juan," according to the Moscow press, but someone who kept an accounting system of his activities. There were no fewer than 521 girls' names in his ledger, in which he made note of address, age, and details of physical characteristics. Ladnov's ladies (the press persisted in referring to them as "victims") were largely students, office girls, and, occasionally, working women, and the official line taken in chastising them journalistically was that they were unable to make a clear Marxist distinction between "high passion and low feelings." For dispersing his energies with such evident free enterprise, Ladnov was sentenced to ten years in jail.

These are only a few brief examples of the kinds of inner stress (or outer rapture) that appear with some frequency on the normally "correct" surface of Soviet life.

"Communist Morals"

The Communist man, according to the official dream, is expected to be one who functions on the moral level with a kind of stainless-steel integrity. Such official expectations, like other federal norms, are some distance from human reality.

The Russian boy and the Russian girl are not immersed in the relentless public sexuality of the West. Creamy-thighed girls do not beckon invitingly from billboards, there are no blatantly erotic movies, magazine stories, or other literature. His society encourages the Russian youth to more rational activities. And there, perhaps, is one of the reasons why the relations between the sexes in the Soviet Union has lately been causing some obvious concern.

In its official attitudes, the Soviet Government tends to take a puritanical view of the relations between the sexes. "Communist morals," as they are called, make it difficult to carry out any education in matters of sex. The Leningrad doctor Pavel Bul is one of the very rare Don Quixotes who is fighting to introduce sex education into the schools. He has told me of many cases in which sexual ignorance has led to injury, to ruined lives, to suicide and other tragedy. But the solutions to such problems do not come, ordinarily, from books.

It is only in the last few years that some rather dreary instructional booklets have made their appearance. Still largely unresolved is the difficulty faced by many young people in search of facts about questions that go back to Adam and Eve. The results, in many cases, are not too hard to imagine. I am not speaking now of the minority of the more advanced members of the Soviet population but of the great mass of men and women. The Russians are not a sexually inhibited people, but they tend to be shy and even prudish about public expressions of sex, whether in word or action.

It is easy to find signs of this holding back of sexual energy in public. As a casual instance, modern Russia lags far behind such more advanced countries as England, France, and the United States, to name only three, in the production of pornography. In Russia, it just does not exist. Also, that special delight of newspaper readers in the West, the sex-crime story, makes only a rare and even furtive appearance in the Soviet press.

A true story will help to convey the general atmosphere: Some years ago, shortly after the late Yuri Gagarin, the cosmonaut, had completed his electrifying circuit of the earth, he was sent to England on a good-will mission. In the course of his public activities, he attended a London trade exposition. On display was an exhibit of Soviet ladies' apparel, and one of the items was a somewhat daring brassière contrived of black net and lace. A British woman pointed to this item and asked Gagarin if "all the women in Russia" wore such things. According to the newspapers, he replied: "Dear lady, I am a happily married man. How do you think my wife would feel if I were able to answer a question like that?"

It is possible that Gagarin was being very worldly in his answer, but it is probable that he was not.

Some time ago, the United States entertained itself with the Kinsey Report, in which the most intimate details of individual sex lives were explored with the willing and even grateful cooperation of the people being studied. Such a report would be out of the question in the Soviet Union. It is likely that any social scientist who set out on such a study would be shot midway through his second interview. Or his first.

Even in the field of the dirty joke, Communist production lags far behind the staggering achievements of the capitalist competition. And what jokes there are, are likely to be rather feeble. Here is one about a letter to a newspaper editor:

> "I am a seventeen-year-old girl, and would like to know what time I should go to bed."

Answer: "You should go to bed by ten o'clock at the latest, so that you can be home by midnight."

In other countries, particularly America, it is not unusual to hear jokes that make fun of women as women, but such humor is almost nonexistent in the Soviet Union. Perhaps this is because the facts of Russian life tend to blur many of the ordinary distinctions between the sexes. Women perform most of the functions that men do, and usually quite as well as men. They talk, act, and generally function as the equals of men, and in consequence, men tend to take them in many ways more for granted. They are, in fact, less threatened by them.

It is equally a fact that the Russian male is lacking in the guile and the use of nuance that are so characteristic of the pursuit of the female in such countries as Italy, Spain, and France, for example. But he does not worry about his lack of such amiable qualities. This is not only because of his own attitudes, but also because of the forthrightness of the Russian woman. She will see nothing really wrong in saving him much of the sexual distance he has to travel by the directness of her own approach. This, too, is a result of her equality.

Even in Soviet literature there is a certain temporizing. It is not that morally unsound relations are unlikely to take place within the covers of a book—they do, but not with any great frequency. And when they do, there is a tendency to handle them with a certain diffidence, even coolness. A man and woman, unmarried, who are having a sexual fling, are likely to be described as "close to each other." At some moment rich with ecstasy, when the drums of the heart begin to beat their loudest, we are informed that they "go to each other." Period.

Such typical verbal restraints do not do justice to Russian love-making, even under the Soviets. A British statesman early in this century laid down the rule, perhaps only for the women he knew, that "ladies do not move." In the preceding century, Turgenev offered to his friend Flaubert a richer judgment of the Russian woman. Only there, he said, could a man find simplicity, tenderness, and "unconscious depravity."

In art, too, as might be expected, the line of discretion is firmly held. It is rare to come across a painting of a female nude, although there are signs of a coming break-through here. When such a nude was exhibited at a Moscow art show, late in 1956, it produced nothing less than a sensation.

The Trials of Love

A woman journalist I knew once suffered a severe shock on entering her apartment. As she stood in the hallway, she heard the voice of her sixteen-year-old daughter. The girl was on the telephone, talking to a friend.

"So you've tried it already?" the girl was saying. "Can you imagine—I haven't yet. Yes—that's it. I'm slow, that's all. But I'm going to ring Victor—I'll get him over here tomorrow. The old folks are off to a concert, so everything will be all right." Pause. "Of *course* I'll tell you all about it. Right away."

With one foot over the threshold of the room where her daughter was at the phone, the mother fell to the floor in a dead faint. Because of this exceptional circumstance, the innocence of that particular schoolgirl was probably preserved a bit longer. How much longer, it would be impractical to speculate.

A major unsettling element in the pursuit of sex and love in the Soviet Union is the lack of privacy. Under the prevailing conditions of overcrowded housing, people are crammed together, with more than one family to a single apartment. It is not hard to see how this kind of ant-heap living can produce discords in even the most lyrical attachment. A young man can not usually hope to spend a few quiet hours at home with his girl friend, even on one of those rare evenings when his parents are out. The vigilant neighbors, with whom the apartment is shared, would be sure to discuss, next day in the kitchen, every sound, verbal and otherwise, that they had detected from the room in which the young man spent his time with the girl. It would not matter how harmlessly the two had spent their hours together. It could be made to seem quite lurid. The boy's parents might then feel forced to forbid him to use the room with the girl unless they were also present.

Even the so-called separate apartments—the number of which has steadily increased in the last decade—do not provide young people with the seclusion they desire. These quarters are very small and rarely have as many rooms as there are people in a family. As a family grows in size, it gradually turns into a kind of walled-in crowd. The apartment becomes a "family communal," in which the older members consider it their sacred right to interfere at every turn in the life of the younger ones, while the latter tend to repay this interference with loathing.

The problem of accommodation is deeply disturbing for all young Russians. Even in the summer months, when the days are warm and dry, the young men and women of Moscow have nowhere to go to do their courting. It is not considered proper to do it on the streets, the parks are overcrowded, and the benches on the boulevards are often occupied by pensioners, who watch most vigilantly over the moral behavior of those around them. Young people will seek seclusion in other people's apartments, lent to them by friends for an hour or two, or in unlit stairways, or in the murky corners of courtyards and attics. The furtive and hasty love experienced in such places is unlikely to abet the higher ideals of romance.

If a young man living in Moscow—factory or office worker, student, or scientist, it makes no difference—happens to find himself alone for a time in his own apartment, friends will come round to call on him on the very first evening. They will come with their girl friends, and will probably bring along a girl for him, too. The visitors will bring their own vodka and sandwiches, because by an unwritten Moscow law the accommodation is more valuable than anything else, and the owner must be spared any expense. After the more formal entertainments, the men will spend the night with the girls, very often with two or three couples in the same room.

In recent years, another method has come into practice. Three or four young people will pool their resources and rent a room where they can take their women in turns, or at the same time, according to taste. Of course, officially it is impossible to rent an apartment in Moscow, but unofficially it can be done. There is a special "market" for this purpose on Shchepkin Street, where every Sunday the business of renting out apartments is carried on. You have to pay and you pay by the week. This is "private enterprise" and the owner of the apartment runs the risk of being deported from Moscow or even arrested for "profiteering out of housing." But for money and for love, there are always people who are willing to take risks. For that fee, you will have an apartment that will permit you to solve the problem of where to go with someone whose company you would like to enjoy alone.

Such a solution is possible, however, only in the larger cities, and even then in the shadow of unpleasant consequences. In the less populated areas, where everyone knows everyone else's business, it is quite out of the question. It is the kind of thing that might lead to social suicide. In such places, young people have a starkly limited choice: either to get married and enter on the painful struggle against the chronic shortage of money, the lack of housing, and similar problems, or to pass the time with a sex partner in the most unsuitable places. The magazine *Health* has recommended a heroic third possibility, sexual abstinence. It recently published a long and detailed article on this subject, which demonstrated—not persuasively—that abstinence is good for the health, and that sexual relations may be harmful.

If you are the daughter of privileged parents, and you have your own room in their separate apartment, then you have, of course, little to worry about. Disregarding the quality of your less relevant charms, you are likely to find a husband with some ease. A wife with an apartment is the most cherished dream of every young man in Moscow, as in other cities. There is even a joke about "marrying windows overlooking the main street." In the Soviet Union, too, there are those who seek to marry into affluence.

But if you do not have obvious assets of privilege or looks, and if you are just an ordinary young woman, you may be in a bad way. The years pass by and no husband may appear. All your girl friends are married or having love affairs, but for you there is no special enjoyment. Finally, you can't hold out any longer, and you give yourself to some man without being especially in love with him. Shortly after, you discover with horror that you are pregnant.

(Here, a word about Soviet methods of contraception: They are relatively antique. The government has never actually approached this problem with the directly rational attitude that one might expect in a nation dedicated to the practical, to official "materialism." The matter has been swept almost entirely from official sight, and only the briefest attention has been paid to such necessities. For instance; the use of the old-fashioned condom, or sheath, is officially encouraged. But the texture of these is not up to Western standards, and they are considered extremely unpleasant to use. They are called "galoshes," and people try to avoid them. Again, the

Soviet citizen on the brink of love cannot choose from the dazzling variety of contraceptive devices and materials available in the West. For the woman, there is the state-produced pessary, but it comes in only two sizes.)

To go on with our story. Your seducer may turn out to be a man of honor and marry you. One problem there is that his parents may oppose it. To them, you may seem an immoral woman who has taken advantage of their "boy." Should he hang on to his resolve and marry you anyway, you can hope that you will be incredibly lucky. Otherwise, you may expect the normal problems of married life anywhere, with the addition of those peculiar to Communist living, plus that of a marriage which begins under a cloud. The bare outlines of this story, of course, are hardly unique to the Soviet Union.

As a more practical alternative to marriage, you may decide to have an abortion. This is a prevailing form of birth control in Russia today. It is legal, and it costs about $11.00. There is a complication, however. Many people will know the facts about you almost overnight, and you will become the object of unpleasant comment. Besides, some of the paper work involved in an official abortion takes on, many women feel, the quality of an invasion of privacy. For such reasons, quite a number of women go to the trouble of submitting to a private abortion, which is not hard to arrange, although somewhat more expensive than the official variety.

There remains, in the story we have been discussing, the possibility that you choose to become a mother, an "unmarried mother," according to the state's terminology. There will be absolutely no official discrimination against you, and you will be entitled to all state benefits made available for any other mother. But there are difficulties here, despite the state's open-minded approach.

Nurseries and kindergartens run by the state will reduce your expenses by roughly a third, but what about the other two-thirds? There is no husband to share with you the cost of raising this child, in a country where most people tend to live uncomfortably close to the margin. Even if you should find a lover, it may not be easy to encourage him to share some of your economic burden. Russian men, especially the married ones, tend to prefer mistresses who do not demand money.

Divorce

The shortage of accommodations, coupled with poverty, can lead to the rapid dissolution of early marriages. However much people are in love with each other, their feelings must do battle with the difficult living conditions.

In the early days of Communism, the procedure of divorce took only three minutes, and the only grounds necessary, according to an old joke, was marriage. Nowadays, it may present problems. Also, alimony is a distinct possibility, and it may prove to be sizable (one-fourth of all the earnings of the former husband for one child, one-third for two, and one-half for three or more).

Such obstacles have not noticeably stemmed the tide of broken marriages. I once sat for three hours in a courtroom, and in that time I heard nineteen separate couples come forward and petition for divorce. In eighteen of these cases, both man and wife were under twenty-five, and in eleven there were children from the marriage. Until recently, the process of obtaining a divorce required that a preliminary announcement should be published in a newspaper Three Moscow papers used to publish from fifty to 100 such announcements each day, and yet people desiring a divorce had to wait four to five months for their announcement to appear.

Another problem for the divorced couple: Because of the chronic shortage of housing accommodations, it is often necessary for them to go right on living with each other after they have been legally sundered. Conventional mores call for them to separate their living areas with a curtain or other obvious partition. Given a little time, of course, one or both of the parties will bring a new friend into the apartment, and a new courtship proceeds, with complications that may be comic to all who are not personally involved. One Russian writer has observed that, in the long run, such a situation can produce great benefit for marriage. When a man and a woman are forced to live together like this, they may—given enough rainy Sundays, their own loneliness, or just habit—learn to make up and live happily ever after.

Such are some of the reasons why young men in the Soviet Union are in no hurry to get married. The sense of urgency is felt there, as in most countries, primarily by the woman. The spectre of loneliness hangs over her life, and it is this that may add to her directness in her approaches to the male. But it is this very directness which may scare away a potential bridegroom.

With such conditions operating in the love market, it is not surprising that a kind of inflation has set in. There are always women ready to go places with a man—in Russia, too, one may use love to escape from reality, at least for a time. The only question remains, usually: *Where* do you go to enjoy it?

Another factor that plays a special role in the relations between men and women in Russia today is the statistical echo of World War II. The war produced a vast number of dead, estimated at 20 million or more, and the greater number of these were, of course, men. The enormous difference in numbers between single men and single women, so noticeable for years after the war, has been reduced, but it is still something of a problem.

Ladies—and Others—of the Evening

The Soviet criminal code contains no article that sets down penalties for prostitution, because, officially, prostitution

is something that does not exist. In fact, in a "socialist" state
it is something that *cannot* exist. But in practice, it is a
profession that is not uncommon in the country. It is not
organized with the corporate zeal with which such matters
are often arranged in the West. In Russia, every entrepreneur is in business for herself.

This is one more field in which "officially it isn't, but
actually it is," and here again, in the Soviet world, certain
absurdities result. There is no legal way to combat prostitution. If a girl is not studying, and is not employed anywhere, then it may be possible to have her deported from
Moscow as a "parasite." But the girls today have set up
defenses against that possibility, and every one of them now
has some sort of job. Conductors on trains, attendants in
hospitals, even domestic servants—these are some of the com-
moner basic occupations followed by the ladies who recon-
noiter Moscow's streets at night. In the districts where they
do most of their business, such as the city center, near the
railway station, and around the Exhibition of Economic
Achievement, the police know them by their first names.
They may even dally with them—free of charge, of course.
But when the periodic secret instructions come through to
step up the campaign against prostitution, a curious game
begins.

The police officer, who knows the girls in his district,
invites five or six of them to the police station. When they
appear there, everything is done to give them a good fright.
They are kept for a few hours in a dark basement cell, a
feature of every one of Moscow's 250 police stations, and
then they are called up separately for questioning by one
of the senior officers. The climax of the drama ensues, with
all actors well versed in their parts. A written record of the
interrogation is made, and fingerprints are taken, while the
girl protests stoutly about her rights: "I am registered in
Moscow. I have a job, and my documents are in order. Why

have I been detained? I was simply strolling down the street."

"But this is the eighth time we've had you in here!" the officer exclaims.

"I don't care if it's the twenty-eighth!" the girl answers. "It just happens that I always take my stroll on that street."

"You watch out, or we'll write down the work you do in the evenings!"

"And I'll lodge a complaint against you—for slander."

"Get out, you tramp!" barks the police officer. "And see that you don't turn up in my district again!"

"Goodbye, Inspector," says the girl with a pleasant smile. "Why not ask me round one evening when your wife is out?"

The girls are careful not to provoke the police too much. They know that these men have the means to put them out of business quite easily, even though illegally. Despite her official job, the process of having her labeled a parasite would be set in motion. One way is to have the passport department of the city police order a girl's registration in Moscow to be canceled. This means that her right to live in the capital is lost forever. Should she try to live there after such a ban, she could be sent to prison for two years. To give a tincture of legality to such a proceeding, the police could obtain from the people living near her a compromising statement, for example, that she comes home drunk all the time. Or pressure to have her dismissed will be put on the people in charge at her place of work. After this, of course, she can be expelled from the city. She is now a "parasite." But as a rule, the police will go to such lengths only in the case of a girl who has really outraged them.

There is one type of prostitute whose operations are conducted with such ingenuity that the police are spared even the necessity of mock interrogation. These are the ladies to whom the police call "motorized infantry." They use taxis.

Practically everything is planned in the Soviet Union, and the driver of a Moscow cab is no exception. He is obliged to carry out a daily schedule in which, in the course of one shift, he must travel about 150 miles with his meter running. This is expected to earn him $25.00 to $30.00 per week. On a normal day, however, it is not easy for him to grind out that many paying miles. But with a girl in his cab, he can easily do three trips of fifty miles each around the suburbs of the city. In addition to filling out his quota of stipulated mileage, he will also do handsomely in sharing the spoils. The girl will usually persuade her client to tip the driver well, and he can look to an extra $10.00 or $15.00 for his daily pains.

As for homosexuals, Russia, like other countries, has its share. But there they are likely to express their particular allegiance with considerable discretion, at least in public. Soviet law sets a penalty of three to eight years in prison for such activity, but in the country of the heart, where individualism invariably flourishes, this fence, too, is blithely ignored. Some years ago, in Moscow, Guy Burgess, the former British diplomat who had fled to the Soviets with his friend Donald Maclean, was visited by an English journalist who had known him at school many years before. In the course of the interview, the journalist asked Burgess, whom he knew to be a homosexual, how he managed these interests in the Soviet Union. Burgess smiled indulgently and informed his friend that modern Russia was quite capable of competing with the West in the more sophisticated offerings of gracious living.

7

THE PRESS:
THE FACTS
ACCORDING TO PLAN

A journalist is normally a person who conveys information from real life into a newspaper. A Russian journalist is continually absorbing the facts of life with one part of his mind, and with another part he filters these facts, delivering them into the paper in a transformed and "corrected" version. The incompatibility of these two functions in one and the same person does not encourage honesty, sincerity, or respect for principle in one's work. In fact, it does a great deal to encourage the growth of cynicism among journalists, as a form of self-defense.

I was a journalist for many years. I lived and worked

among these men, and I learned to like them just as they are—cynical, bright, rather tough-mannered, and rarely free from the pressure of urgent work. They were good people to have as friends.

Here are some of the things that can happen to a newspaperman in the Soviet Union:

The last time I visited Tashkent was shortly before disaster overtook the city in the form of a series of earthquakes. My plane arrived late in the evening, and I had to wait an hour in a queue for a taxi, but at last I climbed into one and was driven off to the center of the city. The good-looking, broad-shouldered young man who sat at the wheel and drove the "Volga" with great verve demanded, "Where to?"

"Scholkovichnaya Street, number 64."

"Oho," said the young man, with a mixture of respect and irony. "The Central Committee hotel, eh? Do I have a big boss in my taxi?" There was no mistaking the sarcasm.

"No, I'm no big boss; I'm a journalist."

He then eyed me with real curiosity (in Russia the passenger usually sits beside the driver). "I suppose you're going to write of the great achievements of sunny Uzbekistan?"

"I don't know yet."

"Ah, come on—you don't know! After all, they don't send you fellows down here to find out the truth."

I turned to look at the driver, but he kept his eyes fixed on the wide, empty boulevard that stretched before us. Then he said, "Go on, you can look at me as hard as you like. I'm not scared of you. I'll bet that if I told you the truth about the way people have to live down here you'd never print it in your paper."

Any Moscow journalist who travels around the country on business is accustomed to hearing these personal complaints. On the first day of a visit to a factory, an institute, or a state farm, somebody inevitably approaches you and asks whether he could possibly talk to you alone in the evening. Sometimes it is not just one person, but two or three, all of them separately, and each wanting to speak to you alone, without witnesses. Often it is the manager or a chambermaid in the hotel where you are staying who wants to talk. I could never bear to turn them down, although I knew in advance that the conversation would be long and fruitless. Some of my colleagues used to refuse, and maybe this was more honest of them. Looking back furtively over his shoulder, the petitioner would come to your hotel room and tell a long story of the injustice, breaches of the law, and cruelty committed by the people in charge of that particular factory, state farm, or institute.

All of these people, who were often indeed being victimized and were usually honest seekers after justice, would invariably begin their stories by saying that they supported the Soviet regime. They would usually continue like this: "But our bosses here, though they carry Party cards, are not really Communists." Often it would be, "not Communists, but fascists." And then the third line of argument: "Moscow's a long way off—they don't know what's going on down here. And our bosses have got their pals up there at the top who keep everything quiet. If I tell you the truth, and you believe me and write about it, everybody will be up in arms. Only you mustn't give my name, or they'll wipe me out here. You don't know what they're like—they're capable of anything." Only after this sort of introduction would the real story come out, and it would usually be quite unpleasant.

What surprised me about the taxi driver in Tashkent was that he dropped the usual preamble. Perhaps it was because time was short—Tashkent airport is not very far from the city. The story he went on to tell me was not a personal complaint. He attacked the situation in the city on general humanitarian and even political grounds.

He spoke very mockingly, for example, about the behavior of the first secretary of the Central Committee of the Communist Party of Uzbekistan, Sharaf Rashidov. In order to sustain his popularity with the people, Rashidov usually satisfied the requests and applications of those who managed to obtain a personal interview with him. Consequently, people came with their complaints from every part of Uzbekistan and lived for weeks on the street outside the Central Committee building. They tried to catch him as he got out of his car, to say at least a couple of words to him or to beg to be received by him. Rashidov tried to keep out of their way by arriving unnoticed at the back entrance, and before he was due to arrive the police chased the waiting crowd away. But the police never attacked people while he was around. This would have destroyed the impression that Rashidov "didn't know" what they did.

"He's our great benefactor, is Sharaf, our czar and little father," the taxi driver said. "But for some reason, it seems that all the other top officials in Uzbekistan, even his closest colleagues, oppress people. He alone is kind—but only to those who have the good luck to grab him by the coat sleeve."

He looked across at me and added: "That's the way it is here, in sunny socialist Uzbekistan. Maybe you'd like to write about it? Or maybe you'd like to write about the way half the population of Tashkent is forced every year to go out and work on the cotton harvest, and then they print pictures in the papers of the cotton-harvesting machine and always with a woman, a Hero of Socialist Labor, at the controls. Or about bribes. I don't know what goes on in other republics, but in ours it's not considered proper even to start a conversation without handing something over. If you want to get your name put down in the list for housing, you pay a bribe. If you want to take a bride, you pay a bribe to the father according to the old custom, and you pay a bribe to the police according to the new custom, so that they don't make a fuss about the sale of a girl under age. Well, what do you think—will any of these subjects do?"

The boldness with which the young man talked disarmed me. I just couldn't answer him in the usual stereotyped phrases, to tell him he was exaggerating, that he was forgetting about the positive side of the system, and that he could write to the papers about specific shortcomings if he wished. I had to be as frank with him as he had been with me.

"No, my friend, I can't write about anything like that."

I waited for another stream of revelations, but it did not come. He only nodded his head slowly, as if he understood. A minute later we drove up to a new and expensive-looking hotel, a separate building standing apart from the rickety mud huts around it.

"We've arrived," said the taxi driver, with a sweep of his hand, as though inviting me to study the obvious contrast. His last words to me were, "Have a good rest!"

Everybody in Russia knows that what goes on around them is one thing, while what is written in the newspapers is likely to be quite different. But this is something they usually don't talk about, at any rate in conversations with journalists. They avoid the subject, probably for the same reason that you don't ask a lame man why he limps or a bald man what has happened to his hair. On the contrary, people whom I interviewed would often say, "Of course you can't write that; that's just between you and me." Such remarks were not made critically but were just a recognition of the fact that there were certain things not permitted to find their way into newspapers or magazines. The rash directness of the taxi driver in Tashkent was an exception, and that is why I remember him.

This must not be taken to mean that Russian newspapers do not print articles that are critical of various aspects of the country's life. They do, and, furthermore, some critical morsel must appear in every issue. If a newspaper were to appear on a weekday without any critical articles at all, the ideological supervisors would immediately accuse it of being "toothless." According to an unwritten law of the Soviet press, a newspaper must have "sharp teeth." It must be continually fighting for or against something or other. But the criticism has to be expressed with skill, and in Russia a journalist learns to acquire this skill from the very first day of his career.

I can remember an editor sometimes frowning and sometimes smiling as he crossed out and corrected paragraphs in the articles I wrote as a young man. He would comment ironically on what he had crossed out, and he kept repeating the first commandment for any Soviet journalist, "Do not generalize! Never generalize!"

I will give an example of what this means in practice. Suppose I had decided to follow up the Tashkent taxi driver's story about the ancient Asian custom whereby parents sell their underage daughters for *kalym*. Let us also suppose that I had visited a collective farm and come across an actual instance of a girl's being sold in this way. I might have established, though this would have been more difficult, that a certain member of the police force had taken a bribe, for which he did not report what was going on. Then I might have visited a second farm, and then a third, called on the Party authorities at the local prosecutor's office and at the court, and come away with a clear impression that the practice of paying *kalym* was going on everywhere, and that it was in fact a public scandal. Armed with this wealth of information, and weighed down by all sorts of documents, I would return to my newspaper office. What would happen then?

The first thing would be that the editor would praise me for having brought back from my trip such "good, sharp, fighting material." Then he would say that in the course of the next few days he would "seek advice about whether this is a good moment for us to take up this topic in our pages." Let us suppose that it does turn out to be considered a "good moment." The editor would then tell me to write it up. He might even add, "Don't be too gentle with them—criticize them right down the line!" He wouldn't warn me about not generalizing, because he knows he is dealing with an experienced journalist. I would write something like this:

> We have just been celebrating the glorious Fiftieth Anniversary of the October Revolution. As we review the amazing achievements and rejoice in the successes registered in every sphere of our Soviet life we cannot, in these great days, forget to take note of the shortcomings and of those survivals of the past still lingering on in people's minds and still hidden away in some corners of the country of socialism victorious. The Party teaches us not to conceal our failings or to try and hush them up, but to have the courage to tell the truth. Only in that way can we hope to rid ourselves of the "birthmarks" of the past.
>
> Uzbekistan. . . . A white mass of cotton, fresh water in the desert, a collective-farm village that dazzles you like a mirage. And right here in this sunny spot, where cotton-growers famous throughout our Union are laboring, a really scandalous incident occurred recently. Fourteen-year-old Tadzhikhon Kurbanova was "sold into wedlock" for 300 rubles and a dozen sheep. Sold, just as if she had been some article in the market!

I would go on to relate how the whole affair took place, laying special stress on the fact that the girl "studied in a Soviet school, and dreamed about one day becoming a doctor or a teacher, or perhaps an operator of a cotton-harvesting machine." Then I would continue something like this:

> I am now coming to the most unpleasant part of the story. There is a police station in the village, which represents our Soviet laws and socialist order. But the village policeman, Sultan Narullayev, betrayed his conscience for a hundred rubles and half-a-dozen sheep. That is how the girl's purchaser (for I am hardly inclined to call such a person a "bridegroom") expressed his gratitude for the fact that the police chose to take no action in this shameful affair.
>
> This is, of course, an exceptional case, quite out of the ordinary run. But it serves as a warning that the survivals of the

feudal past have not yet been finally exterminated in Uzbekistan. From time to time there appears on the desk of the republic's public prosecutor a case involving "marriage" at a suspiciously early age. That means that some Party committees in the Uzbek republic have forgotten about the need for constant ideological work and that, no matter how many tons of cotton are produced, they will not compensate for failures in the education of young people.

Tadzhikhon Kurbanova is still living in a strange, unkindly home, where she was taken against her will. And Sultan Narullayev is still wearing the honorable uniform of the police. It is to be hoped that in both cases it is only for a short time. It is also to be hoped that the prosecutor in the Namangan region and the regional Party committee will draw all the necessary lessons from this unusual story.

I have given this rather lengthy example to demonstrate fully how this sort of journalistic operation is carried on. On the one hand, the newspaper has given publicity to the affair and exposed an evil. On the other hand, it has not generalized about the subject nor treated it as a common social evil. This was simply a single, isolated case, quite out of the ordinary. There is a hint that the incident is not absolutely unique, but the hint is gentle, hardly likely to create the impression, for example, that the police have been taking bribes in other places.

In some nations, the news is sometimes censored, or "managed," or otherwise inhibited from its freest expression. In the Soviet Union it is orchestrated like a symphony. Each musician is well-rehearsed, so that he will produce exactly the desired effect. And in such a symphony there is no need for a soloist.

Here is how it works.

How the News Is Made

Every other week, the editors-in-chief of the national newspapers and magazines in the Soviet Union come together in the department of agitation and propaganda (agit-prop) at the Central Committee of the Party for what are known as "instructional conferences." There they are told what to do and what not to do in the course of the following fortnight. They are usually addressed by one of the deputies of the man in charge of the department. The opinions and instructions he gives are not, of course, his own, but those of the all-powerful organization he represents.

I have never attended one of these meetings, but I know how they are conducted because the editors are obliged, when the meetings are over, to inform the heads of their own departments of the main points dealt with. For my last eight years in Russia, I was in charge of a department on a magazine, and, consequently, I was informed of these "main points" some 200 times.

The first part of the "instructional conference" deals with general political questions. There is bound to be mention of the latest economic achievements, which have to be given front-page treatment: a new electric power station, fulfillment of the grain-delivery plan in the Ukraine, or even "friendly talks" with the Prime Minister of Poland. At this point, the editors are given directions on how to write about various political figures in the West and the East. For example, there was the occasion when General de Gaulle ceased to be a villain and became a hero. One day, newspaper commentators were obliged, when referring to the President of France, to talk about the "regime of personal power," or about the threat that he represented to the democratic freedoms in France, because it is an official myth that the Soviet press stands jealously on guard over democratic rights and political freedoms in other countries. The next day, everything was the other way around, and commentators now had to emphasize the positive contribution the General had made to the development of Europe, to the cause of peace, and to the improvement of Franco-Soviet relations. Caricatures of de Gaulle were no longer permitted, and even the French Communist Party's criticisms of him were to be ignored.

Similar sudden changes, in one direction or the other, have

taken place at various times in recent history, in the cases of Mao Tse-tung, Tito, Giuseppe Saragat, Pietro Nenni, and even President Kennedy. Such turnabouts are arranged simply and unsensationally at the "instructional conferences." Those present at the meetings do not ask any questions. They are too busy taking notes.

The second part of the conference is the most worrying. It is concerned with the various shortcomings of and mistakes that have appeared in certain papers and magazines during the previous fortnight. In the less serious cases, after a specific error has been pointed out, the editor concerned is simply reprimanded on the spot. In more serious cases, he will be told that "conclusions will be drawn later." This means that a Damoclean sword is hanging over his head, and he cannot even approach anyone to present his own case. He must continue with his work as though nothing had happened, until the sword falls. It may drop in the form of a definite punishment, such as a reprimand by the Party, dismissal from his job, or even expulsion from the Party. It is hardly surprising that editors have suffered heart attacks during this ominous waiting period.

What are the mistakes that even the well-trained Soviet press can make? Here are a few recent examples taken at random.

The magazine *Architecture in the U.S.S.R.* published a picture of an interesting building in West Berlin. The caption read: "Building in West Berlin, Federal Republic of Germany."

"That was a most serious political mistake, Comrades," exclaimed Vladimir Snastin, formerly deputy head of the ideological department of the Central Committee. "You know very well that the Soviet Union does not admit that the Federal Republic has any rights in West Berlin. And here we have a Soviet magazine describing West Berlin as being in the Federal Republic. Absolutely unforgivable!"

The magazine *Inostrannaya Literatura* (No. 3, 1965) went

on sale without Arthur Miller's play *Incident at Vichy*, because the censor had ordered it to be taken out at the last minute. That was not extraordinary, but the editor had overlooked a brief reference in the magazine to the presentation of the play somewhere in Poland, and he had also missed the comment, "It was a most successful production of the play, the text of which appears in this number of our magazine."

The editor received a reprimand for this mistake. More interesting was the fact that instructions were then given for the play to be published, so as to avoid any official embarrassment. There is a Russian saying that when your luck runs out, even bad luck may help. In this case, bad luck made it possible for the Russian reader to get to know Miller's drama, which was eventually published in *Inostrannaya Literatura* (No. 7).

One final example. In January, 1962, a trial was due to take place in Tallin of some Nazis who had carried out atrocities on the Estonian population during the war. The magazine *Sotsialisticheskaya Zakonnost,* the official journal of the Soviet public prosecutor, decided to publish a report of the trial. But there was a problem. If the editor sent a correspondent to the trial, his report could appear no sooner than the April number, because, for technical reasons, it takes between seventy-five and ninety days to bring out any Soviet monthly. By that time, everybody would have forgotten about the case, and the report would have lost its newsworthiness.

The magazine's editor decided to prepare the material in advance. Two months before the trial began, he sent a correspondent to interview the prosecutor of the Estonian republic, who was in charge of the case. The prosecutor, flattered by the attention being paid to the affair by a national magazine, willingly provided the interviewer not only with the text of the speech he was going to make, but also with details of the sentence to be passed.

There was little left for the journalist to do, beyond adding that the severe but just sentence—death for all the accused—had met with the unanimous approval of the public. The January number of *Sotsialisticheskaya Zakonnost,* containing the report of the trial, was due to appear on January 15. The trial was due to begin on January 2 and to last for three days, so that everything looked fine. But at the last moment, the trial was adjourned for two weeks. In adjourning the trial, the judge had no idea, of course, that someone had already reported the verdict.

When the trial began on January 16, people entered the courtroom carrying copies of the latest number of the magazine. Each had already read there a report of the trial that had not yet begun, the death sentence passed, and an account of the "unanimous approval" with which the public had greeted the sentence. Both the editor-in-chief of the magazine and his deputy were instantly dismissed from their jobs and from the Party, and the journalist who had made the visit to Tallin was deprived for the rest of his life of the right to engage in journalistic activities.

To return to the "instructional conference":

When the man in charge of the conference has finished with questions of crime and punishment, he is ready for the last item on the agenda. He tells the attentive editors-in-chief what laws, decisions, and decrees are to be passed in the next weeks or months. They will be told that, "A decision has been taken to introduce pensions for collective farmers," or "it has been decided to appoint Comrade N. Minister for so-and-so." They need this information in advance, to be able to prepare public opinion and maintain the illusion that laws are passed "in accordance with the wishes of the working people," a favorite phrase of the editorial writers on *Pravda.*

When the conference is over, the editors put their notebooks away and go back to their offices, where they outline to their subordinates "the Party's carefully-thought-out instructions" for the following fourteen days. The subordinates then set about the task of putting those instructions into practice. Khrushchev, with the frankness that was his special quality, once described journalists as "servants of the Party."

The Daily Round

The working day for one of the national morning newspapers usually begins at eleven in the morning. It is then that the men in charge of the various departments of the paper and the most important person in any editorial office— the so-called responsible secretary—arrive in their offices. The responsible secretary ranks as the third person in a newspaper, after the editor-in-chief and his deputy. But, in fact, neither the editor nor his deputies, of whom there are several on large newspapers, are actually in charge of bringing out the paper each day. It is the responsible secretary who puts the paper together.

When he arrives at work, his first job is to look through the reports circulated by TASS, the official Soviet news agency. Only the four largest Soviet newspapers—*Pravda, Izvestia, Komsomolskaya Pravda,* and *Trud*—have their own foreign correspondents, and even they make considerable use of the information provided by TASS. For all other newspapers, these bulletins are the only source of news from abroad. And only in the TASS offices are Western non-Communist newspapers received and read every day.

On the basis of reports from its army of correspondents around the world and from material in the foreign press, TASS produces several different kinds of news summaries every day. Only one of these, reproduced in violet ink, gives news that is intended for publication in the newspapers. When the responsible secretary makes use of a report from this bulletin in his paper, he may shorten it if he does not wish to use all of it. But he is forbidden to change a single word of the text.

The responsible secretary may have access to another TASS

report, the "white" summary. This contains rather more detailed and more truthful information, but it is not for publication in the pages of a newspaper. The contents of the TASS "white" are intended only for the purposes of counter-propaganda. The "white" may serve as a basis, for example, for polemical articles in reply to statements in the Western press. But since very few newspapers have their own foreign-news specialists, the "white" bulletin is sent out only to them.

Even more confidential reports—outspoken commentaries from the foreign press—are contained in the TASS "red" summary, which is printed in that color. This is distributed exclusively to the editors-in-chief of the few more-important newspapers, and to higher Party officials, "for information." It is stamped "Secret."

Naturally, this careful filtering of reports from abroad, the various stages through which they have to pass, and the supervision by the censor uses up a great deal of time. Even all the employees of TASS, numbering more than 1,000, who occupy their own building on Tver Boulevard in Moscow, cannot deal with everything quickly enough. The TASS bulletins therefore give news that is as much as a day old, and sometimes more.

Journalists tell a joke about this institutionalized delay: A teleprinter starts to tap out a message in the TASS building. The employee on duty goes up to the machine to read the tape: "Paris. May 25. From our own correspondent. According to a report from the Agence France Presse, fire has broken out in the building of TASS on Tver Boulevard, Moscow . . . ." The employee drops the tape and rushes to the window, from which he sees fire engines arriving outside the building.

However that may be, the responsible secretary is allowed to publish only one version of news from abroad, the one lying on his desk in the "violet" summary. And that information will reach the reader only the next day.

The responsible secretary first selects the foreign news that will appear on the front page. There is not much of it, and the whole job may take no more than ten minutes. On the page plan set out in front of him, he indicates where the headlines will go. Then he summons the men in charge of the departments of industry, agriculture, and information and starts to "create."

At two in the afternoon, the editor-in-chief arrives in the office. Until then, he is understood to have been with the "leadership," discussing some particularly important questions. In actual fact, he can have been wherever he pleased, because there is usually nothing for him to do in the editorial office until the afternoon.

As soon as he arrives, all the members of his staff, except the most junior, assemble in his office or, in the case of the bigger papers, in a special conference room. This is the daily meeting that plans the contents of future issues of the paper. The heads of department rise in turn and speak about the material they propose to submit for publication in the following days. The responsible secretary sits somewhere in a corner and plays the role of devil's advocate by criticizing, often very frankly and sharply, the subjects to be dealt with, or articles that may have already been prepared. Then the editor-in-chief himself speaks. His position demands that he give his subordinates a long-term view of the paper's work, and that he suggest new feature material, new subjects, and interests. These attempts to be original are usually rather dreary, because there is rarely anything really new in them. Soviet journalism prefers to operate with a minimum of surprises. But the responsible secretary is supposed to talk, and so he talks. And talks.

After the planning conference, the responsible secretary goes off to finish making up the current issue, and very soon the last, fourth page is sent off to be set in the print shop. (All the national daily newspapers in the Soviet Union are four-page affairs. Only *Pravda* consists of six pages, although *Izvestia* occasionally appears with as many as six pages.) The editor-in-chief then settles down to reading through the completed paper, while the telephone starts to ring in the office of the responsible secretary. The censor is informing him about "certain questions" he has concerning some of the material.

A good responsible secretary never argues with the censor. He never even goes into detail about the questions raised. He will simply tell the censor, in a polite and friendly way, that the offending material will immediately be replaced by other material of the same length. Five minutes later, a messenger will hand the censor another proof, which the responsible secretary had ready in his desk for just such an emergency. Later, when the opportunity occurs, the responsible secretary will say to the man in charge of the affected department, "Listen, the censor cut something out of that report of yours. Go and have a talk with him and see what's wrong. I've taken it out of this issue for the time being. If you get his okay, I'll put it in tomorrow."

Finally, the day's issue is adorned with the signature of the editor-in-chief and then with the censor's stamp: "Approved for printing." The members of the staff go home, and only an assistant of the responsible secretary and another censor remain on duty. Late in the evening, when the first copy of the paper comes off press, the censor will put a second stamp on it: "Approved for distribution." The machines then start to print the issue.

The day's program and the general pace of the work are different, of course, on weekly publications, and even more so on monthlies. But there is one thing that is absolutely inescapable in any Soviet publication, whether it is a newspaper, a magazine, or a printed book. That one thing is censorship.

Glavlit

Censorship represents, in a way, the supreme achievement of Soviet efficiency. In the midst of any disorganization or even disorder, it alone will operate with absolute and unchanging precision. Not a single thing can be printed in the Soviet Union, whether it be a book or a postage stamp, a newspaper or a label for a bottle, a magazine or a candy-wrapper, unless it has been approved by the censor. No radio transmission is beamed, no exhibition is opened for public view until an official stamp has approved it.

On the sixth floor of the building that houses the Ministry of Electric Power in Moscow are the offices of a strange organization with a double name. At street level, there is a sign saying, "Head Office for the Protection of State Secrets in the Press, Attached to the State Committee for the Press, Attached to the Council of Ministers of the U.S.S.R." But upstairs, on the quiet sixth floor, where the visitor sees only a heavy door leading into the apartments, a small window for handing in documents, and a telephone kiosk, there is another, briefer sign. It says, "Glavlit U.S.S.R." The word "glavlit" does not exist in the Russian language. It is an abbreviated name surviving from the 1920's, and it means something like "head office for literature." But neither the first nor the second title has anything to do with what really goes on inside the office, because Glavlit does not control simply the press and literature, but also radio, television, public exhibitions, and so forth. Behind the door labeled Glavlit are the headquarters of Soviet censorship.

I was in this office many times, because our magazine was considered to be an important one and was under the supervision of a group of Glavlit's senior censors. Every time I went there, I had to have a separate pass ordered for me in advance by telephone. When I went through the door on the sixth floor, I would be confronted by an armed policeman, to whom I had to show my identity card. He would then give me a pass, while asking, "Whom are you going to see?" On giving the censor's name, I would be told, "Room number 28, straight on and then to the left." He was telling me how to get to the room in question and was also reminding me that it would not be advisable to enter any other rooms.

A solemn silence reigns in the corridors of Glavlit. On the doors of the offices are little name plates identifying the occupants but giving no indication of the duties they perform. Behind one such door is the head censor, Pavel Romanov.

There are not a great many people who work in those offices, perhaps no more than 100 altogether. The staff consists of Romanov himself, his secretaries and assistants, his three deputies, the inevitable personnel department, and a few dozen senior censors. But the total number of censors in the country as a whole is enormous, and difficult to estimate even roughly.

In practice, there are groups of censors—at least two and generally more—working in the offices of every national newspaper and of all regional papers, and of the papers of each republic. Similar groups work in all the country's book-publishing enterprises. In addition, all printing works of any importance, all radio and television studios, and the offices of TASS and the Novosti agency* have their own censors. But, apart from that, Glavlit is in charge of the widespread "local network." Each small town and local center has a representative of Glavlit, who supervises the work of the local newspaper and everything turned out by the local printing works.

If an article contains even the briefest reference to military matters, it also needs the stamp of the Military Censorship, the only censorship department in the U.S.S.R. that calls itself by its proper name. When the Military Censor passes an article, he stamps the first page with the following somewhat limited approval: "There is no objection to this material

---

* *Novosti* is a comparatively new agency, designed to supplement the work of TASS, chiefly by providing feature material, which it also tries to place in the world press.

being published as far as matters of a military nature are concerned. See our comments on pages . . . . On all other aspects of the article, permission to publish must be given by representatives of Glavlit. Signed . . . . Military Censor."

We journalists found Military Censorship by far the easiest to deal with. In the first place, it worked speedily. You received a reply on the third day, whatever the length of the article. In the second place, strange as it may seem, it is the most liberal of the censors. The people who work there are apparently qualified specialists, who know exactly what can and what cannot be said. And they are not crushed by the well-known motto of the timid bureaucrat, "It is safer to ban than to permit."

The list of organizations concerned with censorship is, alas, still not complete. The atomic and space programs also have their own separate and official censors. Yet another censorship organization belongs to the Committee for State Security (KGB). Fortunately, journalists do not often have to refer to this one, because it operates mainly in the case of articles that deal with spies or with the work of the security apparatus.

All of this provides an idea of the machinery that operates to ensure that not a single word of heresy gets through to the Russian reader. The remarkable fact is that this vast and complex organization works completely behind the scenes, removed from the public gaze. In all the years since the establishment of the Soviet regime, there has never been published the slightest hint that censorship exists in the U.S.S.R., and it is never mentioned in any speech.

In one respect, the censorship authorities are absolutely unbending. In no circumstances will they have personal contact with the author of a work submitted to them. According to the rules of the game, the author must not even know that his article, commentary, or novel has to be submitted to the censor. Any instructions about altering or deleting material at the censor's behest must be communicated to the writer as if they came from the editor of the publishing house.

In this connection, I once had an unforgettable experience. I had written an article for a popular-science magazine other than the one on which I worked. The censor raised certain questions in connection with the article. The magazine's subeditor, an inexperienced young man, was unable to deal with them, and kept telephoning me and asking, "Where did you get that from?" and "What is the source of your information?" I would answer all his questions patiently, but the matter dragged on.

Then I had an idea. I realized that the censor with whom he was dealing was the same man with whom I had dealings as editor of my own magazine, and I was on the friendliest terms with him (to be on good terms with the censor is every editor's main concern). I immediately telephoned him, asked him to see me, arrived in his office, and was given the usual warm welcome. But the moment this intelligent and agreeable person realized that I had come to see him not as an editor of my own magazine, but as a contributor to another magazine, he became another man. Blushing and avoiding my eyes, he said that he was not in a position to discuss the article with me, since that would be a grave breach of his instructions. My arguments made no difference, but only annoyed him more.

I used to enjoy asking the censors, solemnly, to explain their objections to certain things. In the most loyal tone, and looking them straight in the eye, I would ask what they found wrong in a particular text. In the majority of cases, I knew perfectly well, of course, what their reasons were, but there was always a great temptation to find out what they would say. The answers were always very vague. For example. "Come now, Leonid Vladimirovich, surely you understand?" Or, "You just think over the sense of that sentence and you yourself will realize what is wrong." That was the usual type of answer.

A highly placed censor, a friend of mine, once put it this way: "Political sense is something you have to have, my dear boy. It's a matter of smell." This sort of sixth sense, this ability of the censor to detect the right political line at any given moment, receives more practical support at the special seminars that each of them has to attend practically every week.

There is only one magazine in the Soviet Union that does not have to pass through the Glavlit censorship. It comes out six times a year, with a circulation of 25,000 copies, and is distributed abroad as well as in Russia. This unique publication is called *Sovietisch Heimland* (The Soviet Motherland)— and it is published in Yiddish. When, in about 1960, it was decided to revive at least one Jewish publication as a form of counterpropaganda, the necessary staff members and writers were quickly found. But Romanov, the head of Glavlit, was then confronted with a very unusual problem: What about the censor? All the material written for the magazine was in Yiddish. To have it translated into Russian especially for censorship would have involved a great deal of work. Also, this system might not be reliable; in the course of translation, important changes of sense or meaning might creep in. To teach the Yiddish language to one of the censors would have taken years. And to appoint a Yiddish-speaking Jew to be a censor in Glavlit was also out of the question.

The final decision was a shrewd one. The man who was to be editor-in-chief of the new magazine, Aaron Vergelis, was summoned to what was then the ideological department of the Central Committee and spoken to in roughly these terms: "We have complete confidence in you, Comrade Vergelis, and we would like you to be not only editor of the magazine but its censor as well. Here is your list of censorable items, and here is your rubber stamp with your personal number. We hope you will appreciate the great responsibility the Party is placing on your shoulders."

Aaron Vergelis now must read his magazine twice. After

the first reading, he puts his signature to it as its editor. Then he checks through the issue as its censor. When he has done that, he puts his stamp on it and sends the master copy off to Glavlit for their files. I should add that friends of mine who work on this magazine have often said they would rather have to deal with the strictest of censors than with Vergelis. Thus does this journalist lead an obviously double life. In a way, it symbolizes the double life led by every journalist in the Soviet Union.

Professionals All

On Suvorov Boulevard in Moscow stands the Central House of the Journalist, the club in which the people who work on newspapers and magazines, in the news agencies and radio, and in publishing offices gather every evening. It is an old mansion that once belonged to a rich merchant by the name of Postnov. Although not very large, it is very pleasant inside. When Khrushchev's son-in-law, Aleksei Adzhubei, was Secretary of the Union of Journalists, he had the interior completely redone, so that the old-fashioned exterior now conceals completely modern and attractively decorated rooms.

There is always something going on in the journalists' club. There are concerts practically every day in the small but very beautiful concert hall, and there are always films to be seen, sometimes the sort that are never shown in cinemas open to the public. The chess room downstairs is usually full of players and spectators. In other rooms, there are groups of people studying foreign languages, while the women are busy with dressmaking or modeling new hats. From time to time, the club is used for meetings of what are called "creative sections," at which journalists dealing with similar topics gather to discuss their professional problems. I was, for example, vice-chairman of the section for scientific journalists.

But the main attraction at the journalists' club is its restaurant and three cosy little bars where you can drink and talk with your friends to your heart's content. There are no public bars in Moscow, and the restaurants don't allow you merely to drink or to talk. You cannot simply sit around in them—you must be continually ordering something, because every waiter has his "plan" to fulfill. But at the journalists' club, nobody chases you from your table with angry looks. On the contrary, you are known and are welcome there. It is a sort of oasis, even, one might say, a Western-style oasis, in Moscow.

It is there, in the friendly and not entirely sober atmosphere of the journalists' bar, that masks are frequently cast aside in the evening. In the first stage of liquefied lightness, my colleagues may start to criticize their editors. Then they may turn gradually to inveighing against the country's political regime as a whole. In the final stage, when they are really drunk, they may indulge in some devastating self-criticism.

I knew one man, who wrote commentaries on international affairs for a major newspaper, who had acquired the habit of spending his evenings in the club commenting on what he had written in the course of the day. His commentary was usually cynical and always interesting. Whatever his state of drunkenness, he never raised his voice. In fact, he had no need to raise it. He was really talking to himself, and the only thing that seemed to matter was that his drinking partner should not be a police informer.

"I really tore the stupid Americans to shreds this morning," a foreign affairs commentator said to me one evening. "I held them up to shame for escalating the war in Vietnam. What idiots they are in Washington! Rotten humanists in white gloves! They want to hold Communism back, the fools. But it doesn't have to be stopped; it needs to be squashed. But they don't understand, not a damned thing! The only fellow they ever had who understood what a cowardly bunch of jackals all these Stalins and Khrushchevs and Maos and Hos are was John Foster Dulles, may his soul rest in peace. He knew that you can talk with Communists pleasantly and politely, just as long as you hold a gun to their heads. Then they are quiet and peaceful, as smooth as can be. But any other approach is useless; they'll snap at you whatever you say. They are simply jackals, always hovering between bravado and cowardice. I well remember how scared they were of Dulles—those guys at the top. They were simply trembling with fright, though they did their best not to show it. Drink up."

We each downed a glass of cognac.

"After Dulles there was one occasion when Kennedy talked to them the right way—that was over Cuba. And they bolted right away, with their tails between their legs. You'd think that would have showed them how you have to talk. But no —once again it's all softness and sweet talk—dear Communists, let's come to terms. And we, of course, simply bark at them. That's what I've been doing this morning—barking at them. Saying: Shame on the American barbarians. Let the gentlemen in the Pentagon not think that our patience is unlimited. Oh, what strong feelings!

"I read all these people like Alsop, Lippmann, and Pearson, and not one of these pundits who is smart enough to say straight out: Tell the Russians to go to hell and get on with the job in Vietnam. The Russians won't dare to raise a finger against you. They're scared to death. And the Chinese won't touch you either. But they'll make a terrible lot of noise. All you have to do is snap back at them properly and quietly, as Dulles did, and they'll shut up. They'll be begging for peace themselves. How stupid life is. We can't *write* what we think, but they can't *do* what we think either. They are afraid of their own left-wingers. I've been there, I know."

Another glass was swigged down, and his next phase began.

"You know, you and I are really revolting creatures. I hope you're not offended? I know I'm no good—and you're no better. You write about the great achievements of Soviet science, and I write about Soviet peace-loving foreign policy. And in return we are allowed to sit here and smoke American cigarettes. Or have a trip to Paris, to be horrified by bourgeois decadence. Drink up!"

I can remember another of his evening commentaries.

"Do you know what is meant by 'Central Germany'? You don't? Read my stuff tomorrow, then. I've given those cheeky nationalists in Bonn a good going-over for calling the East German Democratic Republic 'Central Germany.' What they are hinting at is that *East* Germany is over on the other side of the Oder and Neisse. Damned aggressors. While I was writing I thought to myself; what would have happened if, God spare us, Hitler had won the war? He was the most horrible of creatures and I fought against him, but I'm just using it as an example—what would have happened? Supposing they had driven us back behind the Urals, they would have set up in European Russia some puppet 'National-Socialist Russian State' and they would simply have grabbed the Ukraine, Belorussia and the Baltic states for themselves. And what would we have called that 'Russian State'? Obviously 'Central Russia,' so as to let everybody know where Western Russia was to be found."

We were silent for a while, took another drink and then he started up again, as though on another subject:

"I was in Poland a month ago. I went down to Wroclaw, that used to be called Breslau. Now there's an interesting thing: It's the only place in the whole camp of peace and socialism where it's easy to find an apartment. The Poles don't go there; they don't seem to want to return to the ancient Polish lands. Laws have been passed giving higher wages and all sorts of special privileges to people who were there, but still they don't want to go. They are stupid folk, those Poles. We'd like to have Lvov and Brest-Litovsk, they say, they really do belong to Poland, but Wroclaw—no thank you. It's curious, isn't it?

"Here's something else: A colleague of mine, an East German commentator, came here recently from Berlin. 'I want,' he said, 'to have your advice. We have certain problems in our propaganda when it comes to the Eastern frontiers. I know the arguments to the effect that Breslau and Liegnitz and Landsberg and Danzig and even Stettin were Polish at some time or other, so that's not too difficult to explain. But what arguments would you advise me to use about Königsberg, Tilsit, Insterburg, and East Prussia as a whole? It is difficult to explain to the people of the East German Democratic Republic why those places belong to Russia if the U.S.S.R. stands for the principle of ancient possession and national ownership.'

"I eyed him carefully and asked myself whether the son of a bitch was making fun of me or whether he was just stupid. But he sat there looking at me, his pencil at the ready, waiting for me to explain how best to tell lies. I told him quietly that it was simply, Comrade, a result of Hitler's aggression and that he should apply to the agit-prop department for the current arguments about it. And he wrote it all down! He wrote it down and then asked: Which propaganda department do you think it better for me to approach —the Soviet or the East German? I had a job getting rid of him and I very nearly told him where he could go."

Although, as I said, this particular journalist always spoke quietly, nonetheless I kept looking round to see whether anybody at a neighboring table could hear any of the frightful things he was saying. They *were* frightful, because such opinions are not voiced in the U.S.S.R., even within the family circle. It was the reaction of a man whose mind overflowed with a terrible mixture of truth and lies. He used to get some kind of perverse pleasure, his own form of escape, by expressing views completely contrary to the official one. And, at the same time, he was running a tremendous risk.

I by no means agreed with all of his drunken thoughts, extreme and bitter as they were. But the fact was that he was being honest; there is a Russian saying that "what a sober man has in his mind, a drunken one has on his tongue."

This journalist was by no means an exception. Many things said in the evenings at the journalists' club are the reverse of what the same men write in the newspapers and magazines. It would be wrong, in my opinion, to attach too much importance to this form of protest, and one may even question whether it is in fact a protest at all. It is perhaps no more than a form of unbelief, at best a kind of fault-finding, representing no danger for the regime. My colleagues in Russia are perhaps capable of no more than this.

The majority of the political jokes told in Russia, which are usually strongly anti-Soviet, originate in journalistic circles. Whenever a couple of friends from different newspapers or magazines meet in the journalists' club, it has now become almost a rule for the conversation to start with an exchange of new jokes. "Hello, Sasha, how are you? Did you hear what you have to do to make sure your refrigerator is always full of food? You disconnect it from the electrical socket and plug it into the radio network." The listener then responds with whatever he can offer in the guise of a joke. After such an introduction, the conversation can switch to other themes.

Humor can be dangerous to those in authority, and the malicious laughter that has been growing steadily in volume in Russia has produced a certain uneasiness in the men in the Kremlin. On September 16, 1966, a new law was promulgated, under which a person can be sent off to a prison camp for three years for spreading anti-Soviet jokes. On September 17, the journalists were already telling each other their own version of the new law: The secret police, they said, had announced a competition for the best anti-Soviet joke. The first prize was to be three years in prison.

But the main service performed by many Russian journalists is that they occasionally try, despite the obstacles and risks involved, to tell the reader something different from the official propaganda. They do this with guile, and they do it more often in magazines than in newspapers, because in a magazine it is easier to slip something past the censor. There, it is likely to be disguised amid masses of otherwise harmless material.

Here is an example of my own. I had read, in manuscript, some brilliant little vignettes by Alexander Solzhenitsyn—very profound, very subtle, and very poetic. They had been banned by the censor and never published. I decided that it would be possible to tell the substance of one of these pieces in an article I was writing on the International Chemicals Exposition in Moscow for my magazine. I began my article with the words, "I recently read a story by a very great writer . . . ." Then, after I had told the substance of the piece, I turned to the question of chemistry.

I counted on the fact that neither the editor of the magazine nor the censor would inquire whose story I had read; I had written that he was "a very great writer," and it would have been awkward for them to betray ignorance. After all, it might have been written by Tolstoy, and it is assumed that an educated person in the Soviet Union must know the Russian classics almost by heart. The article was printed exactly as I had written it, and it was especially gratifying for me to learn that, a few weeks later, Solzhenitsyn himself had read it.

There are, of course, among Russian journalists, men of quite different character—the typical Party officials, the careerists, and the dangerous types who collaborate with the secret police. Many such are to be found in TASS and in the Novosti agency, and, for some reason or other, in the radio field. But they are not in a majority. Most of the people working in the Soviet press are at least discontented with having to tell lies every day in return for special privileges. Their real opinion of the truthfulness of the press in the U.S.S.R. is best revealed in a fanciful journalistic anecdote.

It is announced that there is to be complete freedom in the U.S.S.R., with a variety of political parties, newspapers with various political points of view, free enterprise, and so forth. A journalist sits down in a privately owned café, and says:

"Waiter, bring me a cup of coffee and a Communist newspaper."

"You can have coffee with pleasure, sir, but we do not have any Communist newspapers in this cafe."

"I want a cup of coffee and a Communist newspaper!"

"I'm sorry, sir, we don't keep Communist newspapers in our cafe."

"Give me a cup of coffee and a Communist newspaper!"

"I'm telling you, *there are no Communist papers!*"

"Yes, that's fine: I just want you to keep on saying it."

8

 VODKA AND OTHER
PROBLEMS

On September 9, 1966, *Izvestia* published what could be
called "The Drinker's Manifesto":

> In our country, people drink because of sadness and joy, and
> because they are on a date. They drink because they have just
> been paid. They drink because there's a frost, or because a
> child has just been born. If there are no children who have
> just been born, they drink anyway. Some people drink because
> they are still mourning over the last war, some because they
> feel cold, and some because they have just taken a bath. Some
> drink when relatives gather together, or when a pig has been

killed. And some even start the celebration of Woman's Day with drinks.

People drink a great deal in the Soviet Union, although somewhat less per capita than they do in the United States. They tend to do it somewhat more publicly there, though, and also more spectacularly. There are no statistics on alcoholism in Russia, but it is a spectre that appears to be continually haunting the authorities. Here is *Pravda* on August 24, 1966, discussing reports of whole groups of people out in Novosibirsk who apparently "have no distraction except vodka." The paper is talking about a young worker of excellent reputation around the shop: "Ivan has no amusements. He doesn't go fishing or hunting, and he doesn't even go out of town to relax. He never goes to see a play, and you can't even drag him to a film. He is interested in only one hobby—vodka." The story continues to make some alarming observations about the general drift of social life in that great Siberian city. Those who specialize in the study of such problems have come up with the judgment that "approximately one out of four of all workers in the city arrives at his work inadequately rested. The major reason for this is that he has probably spent his free time in a drinking bout, in the course of which he ended up in one of the area 'sobering stations.' "

The reasons why Russians drink are not to dissimilar from those that cause people to drink in many other countries. The consequences, both social and material, of such widespread drinking have caused the government to engage in a campaign of official discouragement. Vodka has been made expensive to buy, so that anyone really interested in getting drunk will presumably have to spend dearly to earn that elusive privilege. Such official discouragement is no more successful than was the American attempt, with Prohibition shortly after World War I, to tamper with this escape mechanism of human nature. The Russians, too, are known to maintain illicit devices for the distilling of liquor at home. This is especially the case in less populated areas, such as the rural and agricultural regions, where the harshness of everyday life makes it imperative for many people to feel a sense of inner sunlight now and then. They are able to do this with homemade liquor, despite the fact that the quality and taste of these distillations are usually deplorable. Here again, as in so many areas of the national life, the end is presumed to justify the means.

Patterns of Drinking

Through the centuries, the Russian people have amassed a vast number of proverbs and popular sayings that illuminate much of their conduct. "Never mind tomorrow!" some drunken bookkeeper will cry in a state of frenzy, as he flings across the table to his drinking companions the money with which he has been entrusted. He knows he will have to go to prison for this excess of generosity, but at the moment the price is not too high. Or, "So we'll drink and make merry, and when death comes we'll die," and "To hell with everything—who cares!" These are things that people will cry at the moment when they are about to take some carelessly fatal risk. "Whatever's in the pot, let's have it on the table," a husband will order his wife at the appearance of uninvited guests. It does not bother him to know, as he cries out, that there may be nothing in the house for him to eat through much of the next week. And, "Only for a day, but *mine*!" says a woman (who may be the mother of a family), as she abandons herself to the embrace of an officer or traveling actor who has come her way.

Many desperate acts are committed in Russia when people are under the influence of alcohol. But to see in vodka the root cause of people's daring, reckless, sometimes stupid and even criminal conduct is, at best, naïve. The celebrated Russian capacity is only an aspect or symptom of the Russian character. It has long been established, for example, that the average American drinks more liquor in the course of a year than the average Russian. When I was living in the Soviet Union, I could not understand how this could be. After all, no average American is likely to drink a pint bottle of liquor at a single sitting. But now that I have come to know life in the West, I believe I understand the apparent discrepancy in the figures on consumption. All becomes clear when we compare how people drink in Western countries with how they drink in Russia.

In the West, when the dinner guests arrive, you offer them whiskey, gin, or wine before the meal. During dinner, you open a bottle or two of wine. As a rule, nobody gets obviously drunk under these ministrations—your guests may simply appear to be a bit more lively. To take a less formal example, you may go alone, or with friends, to a neighborhood bar, where you spend an hour or two in drinking. Should you be in the habit of doing this every day, your total consumption, in the course of a year, may appear awesome. But in all this time you may have been guilty of not a single visible excess of behavior.

These are the two main forms of drinking in the West. We need take no account of the customary exceptions. But the fact is that neither of these ways of drinking is known at all in Russia. Some people in Russia have, of course, acquired the habit of drinking their glass of vodka before dinner, and then drinking no more. But such modest types are not usually regarded as drinkers, despite the fact that a vodka glass contains 100 grams, or three ounces. In its most widely practiced form, serious Soviet drinking operates along principles far removed from those of the West.

For example, you are invited to someone's home for the evening. When you arrive, you see a table literally covered with bottles of vodka and various kinds of cold food. The host reckons—conservative fellow—on about a bottle of vodka for each pair of men. This means that he expects every man to be pacified with slightly less than half a pint for himself. Wine is usually provided for the ladies, although it has now become fashionable for them also to drink vodka. The guests rarely live down to the alcoholic norm set for them by their host. This is because they have the habit of bringing along additional bottles. The meager supply set out by the house is soon exhausted, usually long before the food has been completely eaten. It is somewhere around this point that the reserve units of liquor begin to make their appearance. Those who enjoy drinking are able to draw additional encouragement from a convenient maxim of Russian mores which makes it unthinkable to leave any open liquor bottle unfinished before declaring the evening at an end. No one will be startled to learn that the result of such an evening is likely to be socially dire. Many of the men will be thoroughly drunk, some of them in a bad way. One or two may be quarreling, warming themselves to the possibility of a fight with fists, furniture, or whatever. And someone may do something likely to land him in jail.

There would be nothing terribly unusual about this particular evening at home with some friends. It might be just a gathering of people who do not have any special reputation as drinkers. They have gathered around the table merely to celebrate a marriage or a birth, a birthday or a new job, or perhaps one of the country's national holidays has imposed a need to celebrate in a mild way.

Another type of drinking is done in restaurants. There are few of these in the Soviet Union, by Western standards, and they are all very expensive. Should you go to one, you may find that you have been maneuvered into drinking a great deal—and paying a great deal—because the restaurant derives the major portion of its profits from the sale of vodka. The waiter may pursue any policy, from cozening good will to downright contempt, just to encourage you to raise those profits by increasing your order of drinks. Here the arena of one's drinking is public and the result is frequently eye-opening. The sight of someone quite drunk on such premises is common, and it is not unusual for rows to develop that can be straightened out only by the attentions of the police. Every restaurant, in fact, has police agents on duty in the evening. Their job is the same as that of the bouncer in the Western saloons of long ago—to eject the more troublesome drunks.

The Vodka Collective

The real drinker in Russia does not go to a restaurant. If you invite him as your guest, he will go along with the greatest of pleasure, but he would not indulge himself in that kind of treat more than once a year. Consequently, the drinkers you see in restaurants are just those who have dropped in by chance. Perhaps for each of them this is their annual bout. The real drunkards never think of using a restaurant. Here is what they do: Two or three friends agree that they would like to have a drink. They go into a shop and buy a half-litre bottle of vodka. (A half-litre is a little less than a pint and comes to $3.00 at the controlled price, though it costs $5.00 in a restaurant.) As for something solid to go with the drink, they may not bother to buy anything at all, because they usually don't have enough money. Or they make do with the bare minimum—a bit of black bread for each of them, or a salted cucumber, or, if they are really flush, perhaps a hard-boiled egg. Then, with the bottle of vodka concealed, according to Russian custom, in the inside pocket of an overcoat, or inside a jacket, they set off. Where do they go? This is a real problem. Usually, none of the group is in a position to invite the others to his home. Apartments are overcrowded, they don't have separate rooms, and neither wives nor mothers are likely to be openly tolerant to such drinkers' gatherings. Also, more often than not there are children in the room where the people live. To consume the bottle in a public place—in a canteen, a café, a restaurant, a shop, or a club—is also impossible. It is very severely punished, even to the point of sending people to prison for it. There is nothing to do, therefore, but to find a gateway in a dark corner and to drink there. This is also forbidden. If the police catch them drinking in such a place, or in the doorway of a house, they may be rebuked with a heavy fine or even a couple of weeks in jail. The drinking must therefore be done furtively, quickly. In such circumstances, it is not a means of passing the time, of talking with friends, or of having a little pleasure. It is something that must be accomplished simply for the sake of drinking. If the group can obtain a small tumbler from somewhere, so much the better. They might steal one, for example, from an automatic vending machine selling fruit juice. A bottle of vodka can be divided almost exactly into three such glasses, and each of the group drinks his share, in turn, at one gulp. But tumblers are not to be found everywhere. The group may have to drink from the bottle.

Let us now suppose that the bottle has been satisfactorily emptied. Munching their bit of bread, the three friends move out of the gateway to the street. Incidentally, the term "friends" may be hasty—they may well have met each other for the first time five minutes before their drink. In the evening, numbers of thirsty but impecunious people crowd into the shops where vodka is sold by the bottle. They go up to other customers who appear to be in the same position and suggest, "Shall we be three?" As soon as there are three together, each puts in a ruble, and they are now, as the saying goes, "friends."

After they have had their drink, they might well go their separate ways, but usually they do not. The real point in the drinking ritual, it would appear, is the opportunity to stand around and talk a bit with like-thinking human beings, to feel a little bolder, a little freer. So the three men get to know each other, proceeding to tell each other names, addresses, affiliations, work situations, here a boast and there a complaint. As they proceed with such amenities, they may be standing around pointlessly, or wandering slowly along the street. In most cases they have drunk the vodka on an empty stomach, because they have stopped by the shop for this drink after leaving their work, on the way home to supper. With no food in the stomach to challenge and calm the effects of the alcohol, self-control tends to weaken, and thoughts become focused on one particular goal—to get some more to drink. If one of the men has money, his companions will join him then in drinking it out of existence. Should their mutual fortunes permit, the degree of their drunkenness may reach a dangerous level. If they are lucky, each of them will be able to make the journey to his own door without unpleasant incident. At home, however there may be difficulties, especially for a husband or son turning up from work late at night, drunk and penniless. There may be a row, and even a woman's damning tears.

Depending on the quality of the row, and on the character of the participants, it may simply be the conventional ritual exchange of chastisement and defense. Or it may develop into a stormy affair, in which voices are raised to the highest pitch, blows are struck, children run screaming to the neighbors, and perhaps even a weapon is reached for. At the peak of this kind of melodrama, it would seem that the neighbors would be impelled to call for the police. They do not. The wife herself, from the depth of her distress, may appeal to them not to do so. The police, after all, will only arrest the man and put him in jail. In a family with little enough money coming into the house, the wife will usually not hesitate to forgo the luxury of having her husband carried off for a while. Besides, the people of Russia take the kindliest possible view of the drunk. If he hasn't actually broken someone's bones, or slashed someone with a knife, then nudging and coaxing are usually enough to dissuade him from any radical misbehavior.

After that first bottle together, it sometimes happens that the urge to continue drinking cannot be appeased with what money the three men have left. They may then, if sufficiently stimulated by the needs of the occasion, begin to accost passers-by. They may even be driven to steal or rob. This is a straight path to trouble, and may end in a long stretch in prison—five years or more. Only recently the "drunk" laws were made much more severe than they had been, to combat intemperance on the streets.

But in Russia, where there is a less than perfect respect for the police, the severity of the punishment does not serve as a great deterrent. Everybody goes on as before, and the result of applying the new law has only been to send new numbers of people off to the prisons and camps. The others, yet unsent, continue with their public drinking.

All that I have been trying to say here is that while it is true that the average consumption of liquor in the United States is greater than in the Soviet Union, there is a human factor which tends to color the pale statistic—in Russia, people are likely to do their drinking in a more noticeable way. This lack of calculation and self-restraint is a feature of the Russian character, and under the influence of vodka, the tension spring that has been coiled inside each of us by the pernicious demands of civilized life suddenly starts to unwind. It unwinds more obviously, more openly, in the Russian character, with the result that such a person may do scandalous things.

Wherever alcoholism shows its head on the earth's surface, it is, more likely than not, an escape, and this neat generalization is as true of those who drink too much in the Soviet Union as of those who do it anywhere else. The facts of life are hard for many people in Russia, who are hemmed in by many frustrations. Alcohol has served as a refuge from pressures for many hundreds of years. The official frown, which is likely to send the too troublesome drinker off to a hospital for a year, is apparently no great discouragement. People will continue to drink too much in the Soviet Union, whenever there is a part of their soul or brain that cries out to be soothed.

Boredom

In any leisure time that may be available, there are things that may be done—reading, seeing friends, going to the movies, concerts, museums, and the like—and many Russians do them. But for many others, who are not fully engaged by such distractions, there is a growing lack of self-containment that expresses itself in widespread boredom. This condition is apparently on the march and is causing concern among Soviet sociologists. They believe it to be the cause of a rise in the crime rate, as well as of the increase in alcoholism. For instance, this was published in *Literaturnaya Gazeta:*

> This condition of not knowing what to do with oneself is becoming a widespread psychological attitude. It is this state of mind, combined with intellectual immaturity, that leads people into the back streets of the city. It is this that fills drinking glasses to the very brim. Drunken indifference to everything around one produces an absence of control, and this cannot be tolerated, because it comes into conflict with the law.

Boredom gets blamed with some regularity for such things as "hooliganism" and other forms of youthful delinquency. But widespread and persistent boredom is only a symptom of a deeper problem, a kind of free-floating unrest, which may be found in many parts of the Soviet community.

9

 THE RUGGED PATH
TO GOD

To the people of the West, perhaps the best-known church
in all of Russia is that of Basil the Blessed, or St. Basil's, in
Moscow. Almost anyone who has seen a picture of the Kremlin or of Red Square would instantly recognize the characteristic onion-domed spires of this much-photographed church.
It was probably the single most glorious product of Russian
art during the reign of Ivan the Terrible. It was built for
that czar in the sixteenth century and, according to legend,
was the work of an Italian architect. When it was completed,
the story goes, Ivan asked the designer if he thought he
would be able to build another just like it. When the de-

signer said he would, Ivan had the unfortunate fellow's eyes gouged out. Ivan was a notoriously religious man, and he wished to preclude the possibility that anyone in Russia might equal him in celebrating the glory of God.

The story is not true—the architects, in fact, were Russian —but the feeling behind the legend is anchored in a certain reality. Russians take their religion with a special kind of seriousness.

The real religion of the average Russian is his love for his country. There is no point in trying to seek the roots of this love in the traditional prayers and rituals of the Orthodox Church, nor does it derive from the new mysticism ordained by the sacred writings of Communist thought. This religion about which I write is a product of the land and the language, the culture, the songs and folklore, the history and the geography, and even the special Russian weather. To be a Russian—particularly of the European variety—is to be unique, and every Russian feels this. It is something far more deeply felt than mere patriotism, and it is probably the greatest single prop for any Russian government, no matter how vile. It explains why, despite the obvious terrors imposed by Stalin on the Russia of the 1930's, its men and women fought like a nation of heroes to defend the Russian land against the Nazi invader, just as an earlier Russia, under the heel of an autocratic czar, had risen to throw out Napoleon "the liberator."

Most people know that Karl Marx described religion as the opium of the people. Lenin chose a more homely narcotic image, describing it as "a kind of spiritual vodka, in which the slaves of capital drown their human shape and their claims to any decent human life." Today, the official Soviet Encyclopedia carries this definition: "GOD—A mythical invented being." The Soviet Government's policy toward traditional religion is a result of such attitudes.

In many Russians, the conventional religious feeling is

something too ingrained to be entirely destroyed. At one time, the war against religious belief was pursued with a kind of violent zest by the Soviet leaders, and yet the old flame was never quite extinguished. The current rulers have learned to modernize their methods, and the official attitude today, though only quieter and more subtle than before, can sometimes appear, by comparison with the old approach, to be relatively congenial.

No religious instruction may be given to anyone under eighteen at any school or institution. At such places, and elsewhere in public life, the child is subjected to a continuing "materialist" slant on all matters likely to impinge on the world of the spirit. If the child's parents have attempted to inculcate some orthodox religious instruction in the home, where it is permitted, their feeble efforts are likely to be washed away in the general flood of systematically antireligious pressures from the state. The young people of Russia, for this reason, have little real knowledge of what traditional religion may mean.

There was a time when the power of the church and its priesthood was everywhere apparent in Russia. That time is, of course, long past, and one of the more obvious evidences is the scarcity of functioning houses of worship.

The Bogoyavlensky Cathedral in Moscow is certainly no masterpiece of church architecture. There are larger and more beautiful churches in Russia, and even in Moscow. But it is the best of the churches still in use, and in the course of time, this white-walled building with its many spires has come to be regarded as the "cathedral church of the Soviet Union." In earlier times, there were more than 1,000 other churches like it in the Orthodox capital of Russia. In fact, according to popular belief, there were "forty times forty," or 1,600, churches in Moscow, a figure that must have included all sorts of tiny chapels.

I do not know how many churches are still open and being

used for their proper purpose in Moscow today. Probably about thirty. The cathedrals in the Kremlin are preserved only for the benefit of tourists, and hundreds of church buildings are now being used for purposes that must cause their builders to shiver in their graves. In childhood, for example, I frequently visited the church of St. Nicholas, in the Vaganki district, because it had become the Pioneers' club. A delightful little church on Chekhov Street, I remember, served for many years as a school for circus performers.

I was very fond of visiting Russian churches, many of which have great charm and beauty: St. Isaac and Kazan cathedrals in Leningrad; the church of the Virgin's Birth in Suzdal; the church of Boris and Gleb in Kideksha; the Bogolyubov church; and the little church of Pokrov na Nerli, said by some to be the most beautiful in the world. I had the good fortune to visit all of these and many more. Only one—the Cathedral of the Dormition in Vladimir, built 850 years ago—was still being used as a "house of God." All the others had, at best, been turned into museums.

The Kazan Cathedral in Leningrad was diverted from the uses of religion early in the Revolution, and became the Museum of the History of Religion and Atheism. Here the government maintains such edifying exhibits as a special section on the more appalling excesses of the Spanish Inquisition, featuring many of the more gruesome instruments of torture, along with life-size effigies of the victims. But it must not be assumed that Communism makes war only against the religions of the West. With admirable lack of discrimination it sets itself against *all* the formal religions within its borders. (It should be noted here that the Soviet Union has the fourth largest number of Moslems of all countries in the world.)

Once, in the little northern town of Kondopoga, in Karelia, I saw the "miracle of Onega"—a church made entirely of wood without the use of a single nail. The architectural style is quite striking, and there is an external staircase leading up to the choir loft. This marvel of design and handiwork has been standing for nearly 200 years. I managed to get hold of the key and ascended the shaky front steps. Inside there was nothing but the dank darkness, moss, and spiders. Children had played there and had hacked great pieces out of the church beams.

Many an antireligious "campaign" has been conducted since the Soviet regime came into being, each accompanied by another wave of church-closing. The last such wave, initiated by Khrushchev, deprived the faithful of yet another 3,000 churches, and when it happened I was surprised to learn that there were so many churches still functioning in the country.

The closing and destruction of houses of worship is only a part of the Soviet Government's policy toward the church and religion. There is a special government organization—the Council on Religious Affairs, attached to the Council of Ministers of the U.S.S.R.—that puts pressure on the church and on believers through the most varied channels. Alexius, the Patriarch of Moscow and All Russia, Vazgen, the Armenian Catholikos, Levin, the Rabbi of Moscow, and other religious leaders in the U.S.S.R. do not quarrel with the Council's officials and ordinarily obey instructions.

The rhythms of the church-state relationship are carefully arranged by the Council on Religious Affairs. But in 1966, there was a sudden, ugly break in the studied calm of that relationship. In the spring of that year, the first religious demonstration in the history of the Soviet regime took place outside the building of the Central Committee of the Party. Six hundred evangelical Christians—Baptists—sat down on the cobbled roadway there, and asked to present a petition. They demanded freedom to carry on their religion, and also that the schools should stop turning children against their parents. This sort of behavior would not have gone unpunished even in czarist Russia, where God had a place of honor. The secret police descended on the demonstrators, many of whom were cruelly beaten and several hundred of whom were thrown into trucks and driven off. Later, a number of trials were held, and the Baptists were sentenced to various periods of imprisonment, the majority of them for five years. They were punished not for demonstrating, but for "organizing secret Baptist Sunday schools"—a reference to their practice of gathering children together from two or three families for an evening of Bible readings in a private home.

Stalin cherished the idea of erecting in Moscow a statue of Lenin that was to be 320 feet high. This colossus was to be based on the roof of an enormous circular building, which was to be called the Palace of the Soviets. As part of the preparatory work for the grandiose task, on a particularly unhappy night the largest of Moscow's cathedrals—the Church of Christ the Savior—was blown up with dynamite. The site was cleared, the debris carted away, and thousands of people were given jobs in an "Office for the Construction of the Palace of the Soviets." Drawings were prepared, the foundations were laid, and even a special quality of steel was produced to ensure the structural merit of the project. Slowly, to the accompaniment of rhythmic esctasies in the newspapers, the steel frame of the building began to rise above the site where the church had been. But with the end of the war, Stalin lost interest in the Palace. The framework of the building was quietly dismantled—with no comment from the newspapers—and for many years the gray, circular basin of the foundation remained as a sort of negative monument to an unfulfilled idea.

Curiously enough, not only the basin remained, but the Office for the Construction of the Palace remained as well. If Stalin had seen fit to create the office, who would dare to disband it? Year after year, the officials of the office continued to draw their very substantial pay for doing nothing at all. It was only after Stalin's death that they were deprived of their extremely agreeable sinecures. Khrushchev gave orders for the office to be abolished and for a swimming pool to be built where the Church of Christ the Savior had once stood.

The churches that are still open for worship continue to be used, especially by the older generation, and, even there, mostly by the women. It is hard to be optimistic about what will happen to conventional religion in the Soviet Union once the last bearers of the torch die out. The same Constitution that guarantees religious freedom—and it does!—and makes it possible for such people to continue to attend church, also guarantees, with handsome verbal fairness, "freedom of antireligious propaganda." The result of this can be seen everywhere in Russia.

Today, the apparatus and the leading functionaries of the traditional church are able to serve the special purposes of the state. They are particularly useful as instruments of foreign policy, especially in those countries where the Orthodox church has maintained a degree of real power. But for the average Russian, particularly the young who will inherit the future, it is unlikely that religion will mean anything more than the powerful, mystical force that derives from the mere fact of being a Russian.

In London not very long ago, I heard the bells of St. Paul's Cathedral for the first time. They were wonderfully harmonious, but not at all Russian, I thought. I thought of the bells of the Kremlin, and how beautiful they must have sounded in their day. And then I felt saddened, remembering that no Muscovite under fifty can recall that sound, because the bells in the tower of Ivan the Great have been silent now for half a century. I do not know if they will ever ring again.

10

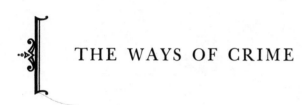

THE WAYS OF CRIME

There is no possibility of crime in a properly run socialist state, according to official Soviet doctrine. To speak of such a thing is to be guilty of a contradiction in terms, as if one were to speak of polar bears in Borneo. The point has often been made in judgments from on high that any crime continuing to show its head in Russia is a carry-over from the miserable bourgeois context before the Revolution of 1917. For example, this fulmination from *Kommunist,* an official publication:

> Under conditions of *bourgeois* society, crime is inevitable. . . .
> The victory of socialism signifies the liquidation of the main

source of crime, private capital ownership. . . . The elimination of capitalism in our country has led to a sharp decline in the types of crime most typical of capitalist society, to the dying off of such "professions" widespread in bourgeois society as the cardsharp, gigolo, procurers, safebreakers, etc. In our country, honest work opens the door of the highest positions in society to everyone.

And here, *Uchitelskaya Gazeta,* a publication for teachers, makes the usual distinction:

The insatiable lust for wealth that is satisfied only in the process of the most harsh exploitation of the workers, produces among the people in a bourgeois society bestial habits, zoological individualism, venality, hypocrisy, and falseness [and] they have their roots in any capitalist country.

As every Soviet citizen is aware, such cries of triumph over the final burial of a major sign of social disorder are somewhat premature. Crime does exist in the Soviet Union. It has not conformed to the traditional pattern of capitalist countries, and the article in *Kommunist* has a certain justice —a cardsharp, gigolo, or safebreaker might starve to death in a short time. But crime has found ways to express itself, even in the Soviet Union.

The Soviet criminal usually lacks the bravura qualities so often displayed, at least in the headlines, by his Western counterpart. There is plenty of crime afoot in Russia, but as a rule it tends to be rather undramatic. Black-market operators are in frequent evidence; there is a marked tendency to embezzlement, speculation, and even occasional swindling; and there is always "hooliganism." Murder takes place, too, but is comparatively rare on the level of individual enterprise. The most widespread crime is theft.

All this, it should be obvious, makes the Soviet criminal a rather small-scale operator. The average criminal is likely to be a lone entrepreneur, wholeheartedly devoted to free enterprise.

Soviet statistics reveal no figures about the number of crimes per year or per thousand of its population. But, speaking to journalists "off the record," Russian judges and prosecutors always admit that the U.S.S.R. is well ahead in number of crimes, leading any country in the world, including America. Those officials are especially concerned about the growing number of criminals under the age of eighteen. And the number of crimes shows no decrease, despite the heaviest penalties in the world provided for in the Russian penal code. Crimes like hooliganism (often ending in bodily harm and even murder) and theft seem almost to have reached the proportions of national disaster.

But if you as a journalist try to write a crime story for your newspaper or magazine, you will need a special go-ahead from the prosecutor's office. There, the story will either be stopped or carefully boiled down. No generalization. No figures. No pessimistic conclusions. Only then might your story be allowed by the censor to go to press. This is why, from the Western point of view, the U.S.S.R. might be judged a country with a limited number of crimes and criminals.

The Free Enterprisers

On the collective farms, which serve as the larder of the state, it is almost expected that peasants will steal food from time to time. Away from the farms, the Soviet Government has faced another variant of stealing from the national treasury. At all levels of the population, citizens have no compunctions about appropriating for themselves the property of the state. This is more than a matter of caprice or pastime—it is considered by many Russians today to be an imperative for their survival. There are shortages in many areas. The government has been forced to deny its citizens many more or less necessary goods, while setting the national sights on what it considers to be more immediately worth-while goals. As a result, a Russian who would never dream of stealing the private property of another citizen, apparently has developed the habit of taking a more tolerant view of the possibility of stealing the public property of the state. ✓

Some time ago, one of my colleagues succeeded in including in his *Izvestia* article the following:

> As I understand it, there are two separate sets of morals. On the one hand, there is nothing more disgraceful than stealing. A person would not take even a sliver of wood from his neighbor, let alone a bundle of logs. A housewife will say: "Even if we leave the washing in the street for a week, no one will touch it." On the other hand, it is not considered shameful to steal a bucket of potatoes or a sack of cabbage from the collective farm.

The theft of building materials is also a practice that causes considerable official concern. Loads of materials, which have been accumulated for the express purpose of constructing yet another group of state-owned houses, are sometimes diverted into areas unthought of by the original planners.

In other situations, too, almost anyone with access to a piece of state property that is not only usable but portable may simply appropriate it without bothering to consider the relative morality of the action. The state, unlike an individual citizen, is the ultimate property-owner in the Soviet Union. It may be safe to assume that the average citizen is easily able to envision that ultimate owner as possessing assets that are inexhaustible. It will therefore be unlikely to miss what has been stolen. Also, it is hard to personalize a state. When a citizen walks off with a keg of nails belonging to a national agency, he will not be struck down with remorse as he thinks of the face, the personality, the life of struggle being led by that original owner. To steal from an individual may be unthinkable, but to steal from the depersonalized state is not only fairly reasonable, but everyone seems to be doing it.

Since the practice of stealing state property is so widespread in the Soviet Union, it should come as no surprise that the officials are able to make little progress in trying to curb it. It functions on the level of a national sin, which is so thoroughly necessary—if not enjoyable—to its practitioners, that they have been persuaded to the view that it does not actually exist or, what is approximately the same thing, that they will refuse to cooperate in any official effort to eradicate it.

Graft and the Pusher

Is there a place for graft in the Soviet Union? There is, and it bears the name *vzyatka,* which derives from the verb meaning *to take.* Here is how it might work:

A man who wishes to be hired by a particular plant is interviewed by the manager. It becomes apparent that the decision to hire him will be eased if there is an exchange of rubles. He pays. After he is hired, he discovers that further exchanges of rubles may be necessary to ensure that he will be given superior reports on the quality of his work, that there will be the proper timing of his vacations, and that he will achieve a better job in the factory pyramid.

This is how graft might be used to grease the path of progress for an individual. It works, by much the same principle, in other areas of Soviet life, outside the factory.

There is also the pusher. He is a specialist at wire-pulling, "fixing," and other activities that are actually illegal. What he may be up to may very well be criminal, but he is likely to meet only the most severely studious inattention from the authorities, because large parts of Soviet industry could not function without him.

Suppose, for instance, that a factory is having a problem about achieving its quota for the production of cooking pans. It cannot achieve this because of a shortage of spare parts. The factory manager has had the requisition on the appropriate desk for months, and yet nothing has come through. The parts remain missing, the norms remain fixed and unreachable. When the time comes to assess the blame, it is the factory manager who may be held accountable. The charge is likely to be "inefficiency." It is therefore expedient for him to outwit the logic of bureaucracy by calling in the pusher. Resourceful scrounging is set in motion, and soon all the necessary wheels, deals, and whatever are in motion. In good time, the quota is achieved, the state is gratified that "dialectical materialism" has triumphed once more, and carefully adjusted bookkeeping at the plant level will see to it that the pusher is provided with adequate compensation for the nature of his pains. Other parties to the deal are provided with suitable rewards to keep them, too, reasonably content. The end, as the saying goes, justifies the means.

The pushers do a great deal of traveling, and it is usually in the style that passes, in a workers' republic, for deluxe.

It is a major theme of official cries to the Soviet worker that it is necessary for him to produce more. In this atmosphere, it should come as no shock or surprise that the man who knows how to cut red tape, to make deals, to get around the barn without waking the farmer, is just about indispensable.

People on the Prowl

Throughout Russia, there are detachments of ordinary citizens who function as "volunteers" to assist the police in maintaining order. These groups are known as *druzhiny* or "people's squads," and there are district headquarters of them throughout every large city.

Participation in these "people's squads" is in theory a voluntary affair. They are formed in factories, offices, and institutions in this way: A member of the district committee of the Party telephones to the man in charge of a factory or office, telling him to select five people to act as *druzhinniki*,

and to send them along for registration at the district headquarters the next day. Along with the Party organizer and
the representative of the trade union, the man concerned
starts going through the list of people on his staff: "Ivanov's
no good—he's too old. Petrov's already got some public welfare work—he's editor of the bulletin-board newspaper. Can't
use Sidorov either—he's our public speaker. Now Kuzmin—
he doesn't seem to have any welfare work yet. Let's have a
word with him." Kuzmin is sent for.

"Listen, Comrade Kuzmin, we've got to appoint some
druzhinniki, and we've come to the conclusion that you're
the man for the job. What's wrong with it? You're a man of
good appearance and strong and we know you to be a brave
fellow. What's that? 'Don't want to' is no excuse at all. There
are plenty of people who can say that. Why does it have to
be *you?* That's easy—because you don't have any other obli-
gations. Listen, what is this? Do you think you can work in
a collective like ours and stand aside from the life of society?
You won't get away with that! Now work it out for yourself:
If you don't join the *druzhinniki* we'll appoint you to be a
canvasser. What do you think is best: to walk around the
streets wearing a red armband and breathing the fresh air
once a month, or to spend the whole pre-election period chasing from apartment to apartment like a madman, checking
the electoral lists and dragging people out to vote? Eh? So
there you are, then. You will report after work tomorrow
at the district headquarters of the *druzhinniki* and ask for
Comrade Volkov. Here's the address. Good luck."

Comrade Kuzmin reports to the district headquarters along
with some other comrades and is told when he has to be on
duty. Usually it is for one evening a month. On that evening, he is given a red armband with *druzhinnik* spelled out
on it, and he is told which streets he has to patrol. If he comes
across a drunk or a hooligan, his job is to seize the offender
and take him off to the police. If a hooligan will not go

quietly, force can be used. Apart from that, the *druzhinnik* has to see that there is no prostitution or private trading going on in his sector, and that there is no vodka-drinking going on in the doorways and under the arches. A *druzhinnik* has the right to demand to see any person's documents for the purpose of checking them.

I was for a long time a member of the *druzhina* in the Sverdlov district of Moscow. I was usually on duty with a couple of friends and, once we had taken off our armbands in some dark corner, we used to spend the evening in a café on Tsvetnoi Boulevard. Toward the end of our period of duty, we would return to the headquarters, with our armbands again on our sleeves, and report to the commander that everything was in order and that there had been no incidents in the sector entrusted to us.

But occasionally when we came on duty, our commander, Misha, would say, "You'd better watch out today, boys. The Party district committee is checking up on the work of the *druzhiny* in our district." We would, of course, understand what he was getting at, and that evening we would put in our full four hours strolling round the streets and chatting about this and that. Occasionally, our conversation would be interrupted. A policeman or a watchman or a plain-clothes detective would come up and ask us to deliver a citizen to the police station. And we would then have to do so. It is particularly unpleasant on such an evening to run into your friends in the street. Some will try not to notice you, while others will make some ease-inducing remark, as if they are well aware of the embarrassing situation. It is much as if you, a respectable man, have been caught in the company of a notorious lady of the town.

The work of the *druzhinniki* does not always pass off as quietly as I have described it. Sometimes the hooligans set on them and beat them up. In a rare case, a *druzhinnik* may even be killed. Should this happen, the dead *druzhinnik* is assured of a medal for bravery, awarded posthumously, with a decree to that effect being published in the newspapers.

The Soviet criminal code can be a harsh one. The possibility of swaying the ends of justice by some particularly eloquent plea to a jury, so basic to many of the fables of the West, is out of the question. The Soviet Union does not believe in trial by jury. The judge or judges, experienced evaluators of the evidence, will determine the guilt or innocence of the party on trial.

The police of such a city as Moscow have an additional club for encouraging lawfulness in their area. This is the law against "parasitic elements," which can result in the enforced deportation of a troublemaker to a locale away from the conventional area of his troublemaking. This has been used to chastise hooligans, alcoholics, and those who are considered to be "willfully idle," among others. The limits of the definition have a certain elasticity, and may be stretched to encompass a wide list of unpleasantnesses not ordinarily covered by specific criminal statute. The police are able, thus, to drive from public view almost anyone they should choose to single out. This law is especially valuable to them because it requires only a very short and formal action before a court.

11

 CLASSES AND MASSES

Cardinal Richelieu, the great French statesman of the seventeenth century, used to say that if he had only six lines that someone had written, he could find in it something with which to hang the man. In the Bible, Job thought it would be a wonderful thing if only his enemy had written a book. In an odd way, both these comments apply to Communism. The sacred writings of that political faith, beginning with those of the primary architect, Karl Marx, and coming down to the present day, represent a vast, almost inexhaustible storehouse of opinions, many of them expressed in the most categorical terms. With so many men expressing so many words over so great an expanse of time and situation, it must be expected that there will be contradictions.

For example: In 1917, Lenin wrote that "All officials and all and every kind of deputy must be subjected not only to election but also to recall at any time. Their pay must not exceed that of a competent workman." In 1931, Stalin took the liberty of explaining what Lenin had actually meant by this: "Whoever draws up wage-scales on the 'principle' of equality, without taking into account the difference between skilled and unskilled labor, breaks with Marxism, breaks with Leninism." In 1941, Georgi Malenkov also amended the gospel: "It is time for the workers . . . to understand that it is now no longer possible to work in the old way. . . . The task consists of encouraging those workers who labor well and liquidating the rotten practice of equalization of wages. . . ."

It is hard to say what Lenin or Marx might have said if they had been around to note these trimmings of holy writ to meet the demands of uncompromising reality. Perhaps, being rather practical men, they would have understood.

There are, today, class distinctions in Russia, although it is customary for the leaders to deny that they exist. In his exile, Leon Trotsky, one of the leading figures of the Bolshevik Revolution, said that "The means of production belong to the state. But the state, so to speak, 'belongs' to the bureaucracy." And those who are members of this "new class," lead lives more obviously filled with the amenities of good living than do most of those who are further down the scale of class distinction.

At the apex of the scale are the true leaders of Soviet life. These are the men who are almost certain to have their apartments—and they are large ones—at the center of the city. They usually travel by car (it is invariably a good one) and have villas in the country. They have nothing to complain about in terms of material deprivation. In this group are the political leaders, scholars of real eminence, and such special types as particularly outstanding men of the arts. Someone like Khachaturian, for instance, composer of the "Saber Dance," among other works, is the Soviet equivalent of a millionaire.

A cut beneath this group, but a noticeable descent in style of living, is the class of men in Russia today who manage factories, projects, and the like. Along with many professionals (here again, scholars and artists of one kind and another may be included) these men are able to live quite pleasant lives. The outward signs of the good life are not so obvious here, but behind the modest façade all is quite well.

Beneath this group is the class of officials who make the wheels go round at the lower levels, and these men would correspond to the adequately paid civil servant of the West. They could be placed somewhere in the middle classes, but the relative elevation there would not be high.

The vast mass of people, as always, are the workers, whether on the factory or on the farm. They battle daily with the realities of trying to make ends meet. They must do this in a society where the norm, any norm, is not designed to be easily achieved. And the norm applies not merely to reaching one's elusive goal in a factory or on a farm. It applies also to the need to acquire for one's self and family the goods and services necessary to make the difference between being consciously alive and merely moving from one day to the next.

The average Russian at the bottom of the economic pyramid is aware that there are distinctions. They are too public to be ignored. If he lives in a city, he knows that there are restaurants with prices so exorbitant that he could not possibly eat in them. As in a capitalist country, such places exist only for those who can afford them. Like his Western counterpart, the Russian worker not only knows that he cannot afford to eat in these places, but he has a pretty good idea of the kind of person who can. A violation has been done here to one of the original ideals of Communism, but the average worker does not really mind that too much. He may feel a twinge of envy when he thinks of the way the men who constitute what is in effect Russia's "capitalist class" are able to live. But he is neither angry nor vindictive about the irony of the great discrepancies in income that exist in a society that, in theory, aims at Communism. Any resentment he might feel is greatly toned down by the respect he feels for those whose status in the scale of things happens to be above his own.

The Russian worker is likely to have an attitude toward his boss that many in the West would consider to be servile. The boss is not merely someone in charge of the worker's present and future status on the job, and therefore the ultimate master of his reward (for which one should read "wages"). He is also the worker's link with the state itself, the public yet mysterious instrument that must be propitiated if it is not to turn on a mere individual and squash him.

In his factory canteen, where the worker has his lunch, there may be separate dining rooms distinguished by three separate grades of food. If he travels by train, he will be able to choose from a number of different classes of accommodation, as in most other countries; in Russia, too, these distinctions are based on one's ability to pay. But neither does this seem any great contradiction to the Russian worker, despite the original principles of his nation's political faith.

In any case, the average Russian at the bottom level does not very much envy or resent those above him in the scale of living. Rather, he is likely to feel considerable respect for the particular talent or merit that has permitted the man who leads the good life to reach that station. A Russian admires achievement and does not begrudge to anyone its obvious, even opulent rewards.

This does not mean that there are no complaints. Since

the death of Stalin, Russia has emerged from that gray, ominous fog of inhibition, when it might be worth one's life to offer the wrong kind of criticism. The complaints today, however, are not against the basic policy of Communism. They usually dwell on an individual issue or condition and how it might be improved. These days, grumbling and complaining are out in the open, but they tend to steer clear of the fundamentally political. Only among such minority groups as poets and intellectuals is there likely to be some questioning of the status quo, but even here the orthodoxies are not usually questioned.

Envy exists most notably in the peasant's attitude toward those who work in the city. The life of the farm worker is the bleakest and hardest of any way of life in Russia. Such a person would have to be almost subhuman to be without envy, now and then, for the comparatively soft and glamorous life led by the average factory hand. On the lower levels of Soviet society, many are likely to feel envy for the important official, sitting in the back of his chauffeur-driven car as it races off to the country. There, one knows, he will have a few days of relaxation at his *dacha.* But underneath the envy is some respect for the qualities that have earned the official these rewards.

If there is any real crying out against the sin of individual privilege, it comes from the Party itself. In 1966, for instance, *Partiinaya Zhizn,* the magazine of the august Central Committee, came down hard on those leaders who were juggling state funds to provide themselves with too much of the soft life on business trips. The cost of such trips was growing every year, the magazine said, and the trips themselves did not always have a business character. Sometimes they took on the aspects of a tourist holiday, according to the complaint. There were times, too, the magazine indicated, when officials were sending friends and loved ones off on such trips, quite illegally. All this was being maneuvered, the article complained, by the doctoring of official expense accounts.

But the officials against whom the magazine was inveighing are on the lower levels of eminence, noticeably below the heights occupied by the current lords of the Soviet dominion. It would not occur to anyone to criticize *them*—at least, not publicly.

12

THE GOOD LIFE:
FOR MEMBERS ONLY

The benefits of power are everywhere evident on the Soviet scene. A leader with a sound sense of the Party line is able to enjoy many examples of the material gratitude which a great nation has to offer. Some of these—the good apartment, the villa, the motor car—have already been indicated. For such a man, life is not only good, but it is manifestly good. This halo of privilege is certainly one of the special lures that encourage many young people to sink themselves in Party work as an act of almost religious dedication. They seek a heaven of sorts on earth. Playing politics is a profitable activity under Communism, too.

When the Gods Are Kind

One of the more benign perquisites of power is the ability to use it now and then to bring happiness to a relative or friend. Those who hold power in Russia have enjoyed this privilege as much as any other. A man who has managed to hang onto the friendship of someone who has achieved the status of a hierarch, will usually have little difficulty in moving with accelerated speed into a niche that is bound to please him.

Special blessings fall, of course, on those who are even closer to the throne. There is distinct wisdom in being born into the right family. Instances of nepotism on high are widely known in Russia, though they are not likely to obtrude too often in conversation. For one thing, most people are quite familiar with the practice and its more obvious examples.

Stalin's son Vasili is perhaps the most glaring example of the triumph of bloodlines over the merit system. A dissolute and irresponsible alcoholic, he was made a general in the air force at an early age. Like an unstable monarch with absolute authority, he would strike ministers in the face, borrow other men's wives for a week or two at some seaside resort, and make similar extravagant use of his power. But people did not dare even to whisper about it. Under Stalin, the people of Russia lived on the edge of an abyss. To talk too much was to call attention to oneself, and then one might be pushed.

At the same time that Stalin's son was achieving a measure of power, stimulus was also being provided from above for the career of Yuri Zhdanov, whose father, Andrei, was one of Stalin's closest colleagues. At the age of twenty-five, Yuri was appointed head of the science department in the Central Committee of the Party.

If genealogy confers no special advantages, a person's merit can be made obvious by his marrying into the right family.

Aleksei Adzhubei is one example of this. A former dancer, he was elevated to the highest level of Soviet journalism to become the editor of *Izvestia,* on the basis of being Khrushchev's son-in-law. With the deposition of his father-in-law, however, Adzhubei's merits became less obvious to Russia's leaders, with a consequent reduction in his status and power.

When the new leaders appeared in the Kremlin, there were predictably rapid ascents in Soviet life. For instance, Premier Aleksei Kosygin's young son-in-law Germen Gvishiani,* a philosopher by training, is now working as a first deputy to the chairman of the State Committee for Science and Technology. I write this with a certain amount of hesitation, because perhaps by the time this book appears he will have achieved more obvious eminence. He has a major qualification—close family ties with management.

How To Be Taken Care Of

All those who lack the visible benefits of family or the right marriage must really extend themselves if they wish to reach the official heavens. Among these people, the strictest adherence to basic Marxist doctrine is not always considered a virtue. This is because the Party line has occasionally been bent into loops and tied into knots. Rigidity in such matters can only be a hindrance; a kind of specialized alertness about "dialectical necessity" in certain situations is more highly prized. What must always prevail in the aspiring executive's tour up the road to glory is his readiness to do whatever is necessary (I repeat, *whatever is necessary*) to carry out the orders of those above him. Time is the arena in which this kind of loyalty is usually tested, and after serving well along these lines, the toiler achieves his reward. For example, here is a brief insight from *Pravda,* September, 1965:

* His real first name, which he prefers to conceal now, is Dzermen—an abbreviation made by his father, a secret police general, out of the names of the first two heads of state security, Felix *Dz*erzhinsky and V. R. *Men*zhinsky.

During the past two years, nineteen officials in the town [in Belorussia] have permitted abuses, embezzlement, and other crimes, and have therefore been dismissed from industrial projects. Actually, however, many of them have not been dismissed, but only transferred to other executive duties.

Or there is this extract from *Kommunist,* in the same year:

In his previous ten years' work in the wine-making industry, M. Gasanov had been dismissed on four different occasions from the jobs he held, for mismanagement and various violations of regulations. Why, we may then ask, was he promoted? Primarily because he had already "served at the executive level." Therefore, in the view of those who were his patrons, he must continue to hold his specific rank. . . .

In other words, as with cults of power everywhere, the Party protects its own.

Even Khrushchev himself believed that there were those who carried this sort of thing too far. In a speech to the Central Committee, in 1964, he complained of just this kind of functional illogic:

I fear that, once home from here, some of us will begin to think: Ivan Ivanovich has been an executive for twenty years. Of course he has made a mess of twenty collective farms, but just the same, let's send him along to the twenty-first. It's always possible he will make something of himself.

Naturally enough, this kind of built-in protective shield for members of the official family has attracted a number of those who are, in the official language of the Soviet Union, "inveterate money-grubbers." In other words, embezzlers, thieves, and swindlers of one kind and another.

As noted earlier, there is a faintly dynastic tone to Russia's leadership today, and promotions to better jobs seem to be made, wherever possible, from "within the family." The new generation of top executives is likely to be plucked from the ranks of the children of men now occupying the seats of the mighty. This is hardly a new development in the history of power. The much-used word "nepotism," in fact, comes from the Latin word *nepos,* meaning "grandson" or "nephew." Julius Caesar's career was not hurt by the fact that his uncle was a Roman consul. There is, of course, considerable logic in the fact that any ruling group tends to view family ties as the best guarantee of one's loyalty to the regime. And loyalty has a prime value in the Soviet Union.

But there are only a limited number of relatives (or even eligible daughters, for that matter) to go around. All others who seek positions of power or privilege in the Soviet Union must achieve them by some more persevering display of worth. Often, the heights are reached by the persistent expression of that one merit that has endeared the dog to thoughtful men everywhere—unquestioning devotion to one's master.

13

 THE TRAINING
OF LEADERS
FOR TOMORROW

On Miyusskaya Square in Moscow stands a massive dark-gray building housing the Higher Party School of the Central Committee of the Party. A mile and a half away from it, on Sadovaya-Kudrinskaya Street, is a large old mansion, the Academy of Social Science of the Central Committee. These two educational institutions, usually known by their initials, H.P.S. and A.S.S., are responsible for training the Party elite.

Nobody can attend these closed institutions simply on his own initiative, although an advertisement inviting applications for entry appears annually in the pages of *Pravda*. People are sent there at the request of the regional committees of the Party, and even then the personnel department of the Central Committee examines the applicants with the greatest care. Those in charge are not very concerned about an applicant's intellectual achievements. More important is the questionnaire that he has to complete; next in importance is his practical experience before applying to the school.

The decisive factor in the information brought out in the questionnaire is the applicant's social origins. A man cannot be accepted into the school if he is a Jew, or if he has served a term of imprisonment in the camps—even though his term was under Stalin and he is now completely "rehabilitated."

In Moscow, the actual process of selection moves ahead on the basis of other, much subtler criteria. When the people in the personnel department of the Central Committee come to consider the origins of a given candidate, they make sure that the potential student of this privileged school should *not* be an intellectual and should *not* have come from an intellectual family. The principal exceptions to this rule arise in the cases of sons and daughters of the higher Party aristocracy. Thus, the great majority of the students are likely to be Party careerists from district and regional Party committees, from the local security organs, and from newspaper offices. And of these, most are certain to be people from working-class or peasant families.

Students at the H.P.S. and the A.S.S. study history, philosophy, economics, and similar subjects. "Marxist-Leninist aesthetics," for example, is the study of literature and art. But the textbooks that are published in the U.S.S.R. on this subject for ordinary schools and colleges are not used here. Their propaganda level is considered to be too primitive for future bosses and leaders. These students have their own textbooks, published especially for these schools—and for these schools alone. Each "lecture" deals with one particular topic, and many of the texts are marked "Secret." Thanks to my position as a journalist and the friendly relations I had with people who taught in the H.P.S., I was able to see practically all the texts, although I must confess I did not have the patience to examine them carefully.

Take, for example, the booklet entitled *The General Crisis of Capitalism*. This subject is studied in all the country's institutes of higher education as part of the course on the foundations of Marxism-Leninism. But for future leaders, the subject is dealt with quite differently from the way it is taught in conventional courses. The general run of students are told roughly the following: The main contradiction in capitalist society—that between the social character of production and the private character of the way the products of labor are distributed—is insoluble. Because of this contradiction, capitalism is shaken, and will continue to be shaken, by periodic crises of overproduction. These will get worse and worse and will lead eventually to the collapse of capitalism as a social system. Capitalism produces, at one end of the social scale, both an absolute and a relative impoverishment of the proletariat. At the other end, it produces a steady accumulation of wealth. Labor unrest is more widespread and is becoming stronger, and it will finally develop into a proletarian revolution, as foretold by Marx and Lenin. Therefore, capitalism is doomed. As with all dogmatic formulations, these are presented with a blunt authority designed to encourage immediate and unthinking absorption. There are few countries in which the masses are likely to resent being told that they are the heralds of the future.

Much of the propaganda designed for internal consumption in the Soviet Union is concerned with making points like these. But the students at the Party schools must be provided with a diet of a different sort. Many of them will become diplomats, or will occupy senior posts in the Committee for Cultural Contacts with Foreign Countries. Others will be in the security services. Sooner or later, practically

all of them will have to travel abroad, to the West and elsewhere. If they were provided with the scarehead view of the
outside world presented to ordinary students, their first contacts with the West might result in a species of shock. They
would see for themselves how they had been lied to, and some
of them might be shaken in their sense of loyalty. For that
reason, the situation in the world of capitalism is presented
to them in a more ingenious manner.

They are taught, for example, that leading scholars, well
paid by the capitalists, have worked out ways of keeping the
economies of the Western countries from going under.
Thanks to the desperate efforts of these "brain trusts," serious
crises have not occurred in the West since 1930. According to
the more subtle line, this was partly because of wars—World
War II, the wars in Korea, Algeria, and Vietnam. Military
orders kept the workers employed and created an illusion of
prosperity for them. Also, the fiscal policy in capitalist countries interferes with too-rapid accumulation of wealth, and
delays (or "delays to some extent") the impoverishment of the
workers. This policy allows the governments, which are
servants of the monopolies, to introduce various forms of
social insurance, pension funds, and other tepid benefits to
deaden the political awareness of the oppressed classes. In
view of all this, it may therefore appear to an inexperienced
person as though the capitalist countries have really succeeded in creating a prosperous society.

When he has absorbed all this, the orthodox student of
the Party schools begins to realize what a cunning and dangerous enemy this capitalism is. It is able to give the impression of being strong and vigorous while in fact being rotten
and doomed. Because . . . and then follow the dogmas
about the contradiction between the social character of production and the private character of distribution, about the
growth of the strike movement, and other themes in the
symphony.

The lectures at the Higher Party School deal in exactly the same way with the propositions of the non-Marxist schools of philosophy. These include, for example, pragmatism and existentialism, about which students at other institutes have no idea at all. In addition, there are "Secret" texts, which summarize modern objections to Marxism and outline the extent of democratic freedoms in the Western world. These views, after being presented, are then exploded by means of various official arguments.

I always had the impression that the system by which students of the Party schools were given some access to "subversive thoughts" was analogous to the practice of preventive inoculation in medicine. Acting in accordance with Jenner's idea, the instructors at the Party schools inject their patients with weakened viruses of anti-Communism, thus producing in them an immunity to it.

All the same, the most important element in one's education at these schools is not the actual information that is handed down, but the special grooming that is provided for the spirit. At every teaching occasion, irrespective of the subject, opportunity is found to instill into the students the idea that they are the elect, chosen to be the rulers of their country. The confidential nature of the instruction, and the emphasis that is put on the Party's trust in them, serves to give body to such an idea. Here, the students are also permitted an awareness of the guilty secret of Soviet leadership: Democracy is no more than the necessary external form in which the government must clothe itself. Political reality being what it is, it is necessary for the people to feel that they, and not the Party leaders, have actual control over the government and its policies.

In that gray building on Miyusskaya Square, and in the mansion on the Sadovaya-Kudrinskaya, the students are trained to present a harsh intolerance toward those who do not accept Marxist ideas as a branch of natural law. Along with this, they are equipped with a facility for editing the facts in any given situation, in the interests of the higher Marxist aim.

The teachers are especially energetic in their efforts to eliminate any of the more troublesome human emotions that may express themselves in a student. They aim most directly at this goal in lectures on the subject of humanism. The students are told that there is such a thing as bourgeois humanism, which deliberately exaggerates the universally human qualities in the individual, so as to disguise and gloss over what relates purely to class. But there is also a Marxist-Leninist humanism, a superior variety, which is concerned primarily with the interests of the people as a whole. This brand is ready, if necessary, to sacrifice the interests of the individual to those of the group.

To demonstrate this superiority, the students are offered such examples as the following: A bandit escapes from his pursuers. It is impossible to re-arrest him, but there is a possibility of shooting him. Bourgeois humanism would not permit this, because only a court can condemn a person to death. But if he is allowed to escape, he may kill many other people. Therefore, on the basis of the higher form of humanism, he must be shot. It is not difficult to pass smoothly from the case of the bandit to a defense of political liquidation as an instrument of government policy.

Representatives of the Committee of State Security (KGB) maintain a close and active contact with both the Higher Party School and the Academy of Social Science. They deliver lectures there on "the insidious methods and tricks used by foreign intelligence networks," and, more recently, the "ideological sabotage" and the "demoralization" of Soviet young people by means of Western propaganda, among other topics. They teach the students to depend, in their future work as leaders, on the security services, to collaborate with them, and to maintain the closest relations with them. Apart from these overt contacts, there exist others, less obvious, between the KGB and the two schools. The fact is that among the students of the Higher Party School and the Academy of Social Science—but especially of the latter—there are a considerable number of young and ambitious Party officials from the countries of Eastern Europe and from East Germany. The Soviet security services are constantly on the lookout to recruit from among them agents and informers for their own purposes. When he returns to his own country after graduating from one of the Party schools, such a recruit is conscious of the importance of the task with which he has been entrusted. It may have been intimated to him that the top leaders in his country are not entirely reliable, that he must watch them closely, protect them from any "bourgeois degeneration," and pass on any information about such un-Marxist decay to the right quarters.

The Path of Privilege

Those who have been through a course at one of these schools never return to their previous places of employment. They are assigned to better and more important jobs. It is a rare graduate who will feel distressed by the thought that he is now, and to the end of his days, at the disposal of the personnel department of the Central Committee of the Party. It is true that a graduate is denied even the very limited options permitted to other citizens, but he is usually only too willingly a captive to these new restraints. He may not be able to choose a job according to his own preference, but his sacrifice has certain compensations. For example, he is relieved once and for all of everyday material worries. Wherever he may go, news of his impending arrival precedes him, and proper welcome is waiting when he gets there. And when he must reside in one place, a home, furniture, food, and even servants will appear, apparently of their own accord, as he, devoted functionary that he is, remains engrossed in his official duties.

All regional committees of the Party have special "administration departments." These are responsible for providing members of the Party apparatus (in strict accordance with their relative rank) with apartments, country houses, food, clothes, free trips to health homes, and even theater tickets. I was very glad to be able to make use of these departments when I had to travel round the country. Suppose you arrive in a provincial town where there is, of course, not a single hotel bed to be had. Other travelers will be crowding the lobby, discussing the prospects of finding somewhere to sleep. But you have in your pocket a little red folder showing you to be a member of the Union of Journalists of the U.S.S.R., and a letter of authority signed by your editor. So you leave your bag with the porter and go straight to the office of the Party committee and into its administration department. There you are sure to find an important-looking man, bored to death with having nothing to do. He will be very pleased to meet a newspaperman from Moscow. He will pretend to be interested in the purpose of your visit and he may even tell you something of the achievements of the local industries. But the only thing that really interests him is whether your documents are genuine. He will study them with great care and, once satisfied, he will ask whether you are comfortable in "our town." At this point you will say, "To tell the truth I haven't got myself fixed up yet. You know, I just threw my bag down in the hotel and came straight to the Party office. But I got the impression that it's not so easy to get a room down there."

The party official may say, "Yes, we're still a bit short of hotel accommodations. But don't worry, we'll help you." And with these words he will either make a telephone call or he will simply take from a drawer a miracle-working voucher. You will thank him, stay a couple of minutes longer chatting for appearances' sake, and return to the hotel. There you will find immediately that there is a separate room for you, possibly even the best in the hotel. If you had not turned up, the room would have remained empty—"reserved for the Party committee." Meanwhile, ordinary mortals would have had to sleep in armchairs in the lobby, or would have gone knocking at the doors of rooms occupied by other guests, in the desperate hope of finding somewhere to lay their heads.

I remember once arriving like this in the city of Gorky. There was a very hard December frost and a bitter wind blowing from the Volga. The thermometer on the embankment, where the Hotel Central is situated, showed thirty-nine degrees below zero. People in sheepskin coats were stamping around the hotel lobby, loudly cursing their fate, while on the reception desk there was a beautifully painted notice, in gold letters on blue glass, "No rooms in the hotel today." I warmed myself up a little, hurried across the wide Minin Square and into the Kremlin (Gorky has one, too). I went to the well-heated and well-lit offices of the Party committee. One-half hour later, I was back at the hotel with my precious voucher. But the besieging mob would not even let me get near the reception desk. After all, who was I to be let through out of turn? It was, in fact, a queue for nothing at all. When I finally managed to push my way through and to show my voucher to the woman at the desk, she made the mistake of asking, "What sort of room would you like—on the warm side or the cool side?" At the sound of this question, the people behind me broke out in a frightful roar of indignation, and it seemed to me for a moment that violence was in the air. I recall one of the comments that was rasped at me: "Every service for the 'servants of the people'!" The man who made this remark was ridiculing a title that many Soviet leaders enjoy pinning on themselves in public.

The graduates of the Higher Party School and the Academy of Social Science occupy today practically all the top- and medium-level positions in the regional committees. They are also entrenched in the central committees of the parties in the various republics of the U.S.S.R. It is they, too, who sit in the Central Committee in Moscow. This elite group in the population—the *apparatchiki*—hold all the real power in their hands.

Those who graduate, in addition to finding their way into key posts in the administration of the regions and the larger cities, are also assigned to jobs in the diplomatic service. Some, too, become leaders of youth organizations, sports clubs, and cultural groups. Many of these keep in touch with similar groups around the world. Other of these graduates are sent to work in the press, cinema, radio, and television. In such places, they are unlikely to do any of the writing or directing, or to indulge in any other creative exercise. Their function is on a somewhat higher level, by Soviet standards —they supervise. And finally, for many of them, the path from the Higher Party School, and less frequently from the Academy of Social Science, leads directly into the security services. I knew many of this latter breed, but it is difficult to discuss any one of them as an individual. As a rule, they are prone to cultivate in themselves something that might be called complete nondistinction. Any personal qualities or other obvious aspects of individual coloration are usually kept discreetly concealed. They try not to have any personal interests, and wherever possible are likely to avoid the more obvious human weaknesses. They even try to dress like all their colleagues of the same rank. In Stalin's time they always wore beige-green tunics. Today they go around in gray suits.

The graduates of these schools have a great deal of difficulty in keeping their old friends. Most of those who were close to them far back in their undedicated earlier years have probably fallen behind in the scramble for success. As a result, these men are likely to fall back into that vast limbo of "people one used to know." The man who has reached the heights (or is on his way to them) is always very busy. He makes little effort to keep in touch with those who have remained too far below him in the scale of power values. After a while, the man down below realizes that it is a waste of time for him to persist in trying to keep contact with his now-important friend. Even their wives and children pay the necessary penalty of the stark difference in status and stop seeing each other.

The family of the higher-up will now mix only with families on its own level. Should one of them succeed in moving ahead to an even higher position, the entire life of the family, including the style of wedding the children will celebrate, will now be carried on in the mode that typifies the newer, higher level. At such heights a "mixed marriage" is extremely rare, because it is the kind of misfortune that may ruin an otherwise promising career. But if the son or daughter of highly placed parents should decide, contrary to parental wishes, to violate the canon on status, then, as a rule, he or she is likely to be forced to leave the more highly placed level, to move down to the lower one, and to remain there forever.

A Love Story

A friend of mine, a fairly well-known Moscow poet, became a victim of these unwritten but rigid laws of social apartheid. He was once invited to a party in the stratosphere of official life. (The tradition of inviting poets to amuse the aristocracy has existed in many countries for many centuries.) At the party, he was struck down by romance. A girl by the name of Natasha fell desperately in love with him. The poet was unmarried, and in the normal course of events such an affair might well have ended in a wedding, since the girl was very attractive and my friend was quite fond of her. The trouble was, however, that Natasha, a student in a pedagogical institute, was the daughter of a member of the Central Committee of the Party.

My friend—who, in the early stages of the affair was not burning with any great passion and understood perfectly well what the situation was—bravely decided not to let himself be too deeply involved in such a romance. Very cautiously, and trying his best not to hurt her, he gave Natasha to understand that they were not suited to one another. He was just a poet, he said, and occupied no high position in the administration. He was not even a member of the Union of Writers. Also, it was not his habit to sing the praises of the Party in his verses, and he therefore had little hope of promotion to a high position in poetic officialdom. To cap all these disadvantages, he was half-Jewish.

To his great surprise, Natasha said that she knew all that and that she understood the situation as well as he did. But he was the only man for her, and she didn't give a damn for the conventions. If he loved her, then she would move the world to get what she wanted. There was nothing left for the poet to do but bestow a kiss on this bold and self-sacrificing young lady.

It was at this stage of their relationship that I was first introduced to Natasha. I formed a very high opinion of her. She was a real person, an individual, one who used her own head and tried to make up her own mind about the world around her. She did not once refer to her parents in my presence, and she spoke only very little, and reluctantly, about them to the man she loved. She always came to him when they met, and at the time, he had not yet visited her in her home. He was not, in fact, particularly anxious to go there.

As often happens, my friend began to fall ever more deeply in love with Natasha, and now their love was fully joined. But there were problems, and he would tell me about them. For example, her first visits to him were strangely brief. She would arrive, stay for half an hour, and go away. Moreover, she would ask him not to leave with her. When, finally, the poet asked for an explanation, it turned out that there was always a chauffeur-driven car waiting for her at the corner. This bothered my friend, and he asked her to visit him in the future like an ordinary person, by bus. Natasha obeyed.

On another occasion, she invited the poet and me to the home of one of her girl friends. This girl was the daughter of a high-ranking general in the State Security service. As a result, at the entrance to the house we had to submit to long questioning about our business there.

Some time after this, Natasha called me on the telephone and, with wild excitement in her voice, announced, "Leonid —hurrah! We're getting married! We're ready to accept congratulations and presents in unlimited quantities!"

I was very glad. My friend appeared to be happy. But his mother appeared to be the happiest of all of us. She had formed a very close attachment to Natasha, called her "daughter," and was already boasting about her future daughter-in-law. I do not wish to cast doubts on the sincerity of that dear woman, who had spent eight years in the prison camps and had lost a husband to Stalin's official fury, but it was apparent that she derived a sensible satisfaction from Natasha's privileged origins. She probably felt that, with such a daughter-in-law, her family would be protected from any further unpleasantness. Her son was a poet, and the natural medium of many poets under rank authority is trouble.

There was only one cloud in this otherwise clear sky. Neither my friend nor his mother had yet been introduced to Natasha's family. Somehow their meeting kept being postponed. Either the father was in Poland or the mother was in Italy or both were in the country. Natasha would smile at her fiancé in a carefree manner and say that they would "have to go through with" the marriage, and he and his mother would soon be invited to meet her parents.

A day was fixed for the wedding, and the bride-to-be spent long hours in the little slum of an apartment where my friend lived, preparing for the forthcoming event. She always went home to sleep, an action that, in the context of normal Soviet morals, evoked general admiration.

But one warm May morning, the bride-to-be did not appear as she had promised to do the previous day. The telephone in her apartment did not answer. After waiting a day or two, the poet went in desperation to the apartment of Natasha and her parents. A guard in the hallway would not allow him to enter the lift, and told him that all members of the family he sought had gone away for an indefinite period.

A week after the day appointed for the wedding that did not take place, my friend received a letter—a few hastily scrawled words, which Natasha had given to someone to post. She informed him that she had left by ship for America as a "member of the crew," and that this had been the only possible way of diverting the threat hanging over my friend. She said she loved him more than ever, but that what had happened was beyond her control, and that she had been unable to fight against it. The letter ended with an appeal for him not to try to find her and not to make inquiries about her, so that he should not get into trouble.

After an absence of two years, Natasha reappeared. She telephoned my friend's mother and asked about him, while evading questions about herself. The mother invited her to come for a visit, and Natasha came. But when my friend heard of the invitation, he stayed away. For three hours, Natasha wept on the bosom of that kindly old lady, obviously hoping that he would return. But he came back only after she had left. In the course of the next few days, he arranged a hurried marriage with an actress with whom he had only recently begun a rather lighthearted romance.

A little later it became known that Natasha had also married. "It's a very long story," she explained over the telephone to the poet's mother. "I didn't want to. I never wanted to. But what could I do!" Whatever else had happened, in this case the parents of the girl had prevented a misalliance.

For the young lovers, the solution was not a happy one. But Romeo and Juliet, presented with much the same problem, were driven to kill themselves. A successful writer for *Pravda,* making this point, would perhaps add that *they* had lived "under capitalism."

14

 THE ARTS:
DANGER—
MEN THINKING

Modern Russia has always had trouble with her writers. Her
great literature is largely the product of the nineteenth century, and was created by men who proved to be—most of
them, anyway—a nuisance to the authorities of their time.
Here is a brief record:

Feodor Dostoyevsky—Condemned to death for political
activity; the sentence was commuted at the last moment, and
he was sent off to Siberia as a prisoner.

Leo Tolstoy—In his last decades, he expressed loud and
frequent dissatisfaction with almost every aspect of the way
in which his world was run. He preached a form of stateless

anarchy, but was by then so eminent that the government did not dare to shut him up.

Ivan Turgenev—Creator of the term "nihilist," he was forced to leave Russia because of his opinions. He spent most of his life as an exile in France.

Alexander Pushkin—His writings, suffused with a love of freedom, were too threatening to those in power. In 1837, he was killed in a duel. Apparently, the duel had been deliberately provoked by the wishes of the Czar. It was a kind of unofficial execution for a troublemaker.

Anton Chekhov—At the height of his fame, he traveled across Russia to the convict islands of Sakhalin, in the Pacific. After a personal survey, he exposed the disgraceful conditions under which the men and women prisoners there were forced to live.

Maxim Gorky—He was expelled from the czarist Academy of Sciences and then became the major literary figure of the Bolshevik Revolution.

No one who is aware of history would make the mistake of assuming that it is only in Russia that writers have been a cause of concern to the status quo. It is a cliché of civil liberties that Voltaire cried out, "I disagree with what you say, but will defend with my life your right to say it!" Because his own government did not share this liberal view, Voltaire had to make remarks like this from the safety of neighboring Switzerland.

Even Lenin himself—a premature Lenin, perhaps, but Lenin nevertheless—might be convicted of giving aid and comfort to the always embattled forces of freedom. Here is what he wrote in 1903, as his contribution to the war on crass authority:

> We demand immediate and unconditional recognition by the authorities of freedom of assembly, freedom of press, and an amnesty for all "political" prisoners and dissenters. Until this is done, all words about tolerance, about religious liberty, will

remain a miserable game and an indecent lie. Until freedom of assembly, of speech, and of press is declared, there will not disappear the shameful Russian inquisition which persecutes profession of unofficial faith, unofficial opinions, unofficial doctrines.

These are noble words, and anyone who chose to cry them out in the Russia of today would be in serious trouble.

The world knows that in 1966, two Soviet writers, Andrei Sinyavsky and Yuli Daniel, were prosecuted for "disseminating material slanderous" to the Soviet Union. Their work had been smuggled abroad. The men pleaded "not guilty," insisting on their right to publish wherever they could.

Much of the drama took place outside the courtroom. For example, before the trial, about 100 young men and women gathered at the foot of the Pushkin monument, in Moscow, and suddenly there appeared above their heads white handwritten banners saying: "Keep to the Constitution!" and "Freedom for Sinyavsky and Daniel!" Passers-by stopped in amazement, not understanding what was going on. The idea that anybody might stage an antigovernment demonstration did not enter anyone's mind. Many thought that someone was shooting a film.

The banners fluttered above the heads of the demonstrators for no more than five or six seconds. Dozens of plainclothes police agents, who had been standing around for a long time, suddenly charged into the crowd of young people. The KGB had known in advance that a demonstration was being planned. With their fists flying, these men pushed their way through to the banners, pulled them down, tore them up, and trampled on them. Other agents surrounded the monument, to make sure that none of the culprits managed to slip away. The demonstrators were seized and rushed into police cars; it was, indeed, very like the shooting of a scene from a well-rehearsed film.

What had happened? It appears that the young people involved belonged to the organization known by the provocative name of the "Society of Young Geniuses." They did not conceal their intention to demonstrate in defense of the writers. In fact, they had sent out hundreds of invitations urging people to come to Pushkin Square. They had appealed to writers, artists, students, and young scientists to support their action. It was an open and exceptionally daring challenge to the regime. The police, too, had accepted this invitation to appear.

Despite such internal clamor, and despite the concern and sympathy aroused for the two men throughout the intellectual community of the world, Sinyavsky and Daniel were convicted and sent to jail. They had committed the oldest of writers' crimes: thinking too hard and setting their thoughts down for others to see.

To anyone interested in running a country in his own way, with no questions asked, it is entirely understandable that such as Sinyavsky and Daniel must be deprived of their typewriters. Here is what Sinyavsky, under the pen name of "Abram Tertz," had been up to in a book (unpublished in the Soviet Union, of course) called *The Trial Begins:*

In the climactic scene, a young man, Seryozha, who has been picked up for suspicious political activity, is being questioned by the Interrogator. The Interrogator probes very gently—after all, he does embroidery in his free time. Suddenly, from amid all this soothing courtesy there comes flying at Seryozha a remark that in effect charges him with having had contact with foreign agents. The reader knows that this is not true. Seryozha thinks that this must be the Interrogator's idea of some kind of a crazy joke. "Please remember, I have not so far been condemned, I am only on trial," he says. The Interrogator beckons him to the window, and tells him to look out into the great city square, below. He points to the people there and, while gently stroking the young man's head, tells him that *they* are on trial, but *"you* are condemned." The result, for Seryozha, is Siberia.

The honor roll of literature under the Soviets reads more like a casualty list. Here are some names:

Anna Akhmatova—Prominent poet, denounced under Stalin as "half-nun and half-fornicatress," prohibited from writing for Soviet publications. Her son was sent off to a labor camp in Siberia, and if it had not been for the generosity of her friends, it is probable that she would have starved.

Isaac Babel—Writer of brilliant short stories. He was arrested in 1937 and sent to a prison camp, where he died.

Ossip Mandelstam—Poet. His fate was Siberia and death.

Vladimir Mayakovsky—Poet, sometimes called "the Voice of the Revolution." His career ended in disillusionment and suicide.

Boris Pasternak—Poet, and author of the officially condemned *Doctor Zhivago*. He was reduced to spending his time at translating, which was for him a form of exile of the spirit.

These names are only a few, picked from among many.

The government, by using its power to render voiceless most of the best writers in the Soviet Union, produced a situation that could surprise no sensible person. A kind of Gresham's Law prevailed. This instructive law of economics, which tells us that an abundance of bad money will force good money into hiding, is also operable in other fields. With real artistic talent in hiding, or dead, the way was open for lesser mortals to bleat their way to official approval and even eminence.

It is too easy to jump to the conclusion that the current herd of Soviet writers is no match for the giants who adorned the literature of pre-Bolshevik times, particularly in the last century.

Those of the good writers still extant in the Soviet Union continue to write, but now their efforts are confined to a largely underground distribution. For every Yevtushenko, who embarrasses the administration with his cries against the hypocrisy of the official attitude on Babi Yar, there are others whose verses strike even more closely to the official bone. These are likely to be so taboo in content that they circulate by hand, copied by pen or typewriter. The particularly good stories and poems in this underground category are able to leave their contagion in every thinking quarter of the country with almost lightning speed.

It should not be hastily assumed that the writers of such "protest literature" seek to overthrow their government. They do not. They are trying only to bring about certain reforms in the Soviet way of life. Freedom of thought and speech are the burning concerns of those who write this literature, but they seek to achieve such freedoms under the auspices of a Soviet regime, and not one that may be imported from the West.

On occasion, a Moscow protester, carried away with fervor, will recite his verses in front of the Pushkin statue. Naturally, as he has expected, he will be arrested. If his luck is bad, he will be sentenced to several years in prison for his sin. If his luck is calamitous, he may very well be sentenced to a mental hospital. Such places have become official dumping grounds for a wide variety of dissidents who bring discomfort to the regime. In time, the patient may hope to be released, unless the conditions under which he has been forced to endure have been too much for him. Then, he will spend the rest of his life in one of these mental wards.

Valeriy Tarsis, the novelist, was confined to just such a hospital. His book *Ward 7* made the charge that a major psychiatric hospital in Moscow is occupied largely with critics of the Soviet authorities, as well as with people who have attempted to depart from Soviet society by committing sui-

cide. Both types of persons are considered of equally unsound mind, according to Tarsis, who himself was later
permitted to emigrate to the West.

For writers seeking primarily to please the men who
make official policy, the joys of special ease and recognition
are soon available. It is possible to become a "millionaire" in
the arts, at least by Soviet standards. The Lenin Prize alone
is worth about $22,000 to a gifted—or prudent—writer. Only
a cynic would point out that today in Russia even the names
of the prizes have sometimes been censored. Originally, this
notable reward was called a "Stalin Prize."

In the autumn of 1965, shortly before the Sinyavsky-Daniel
trial, in the very midst of all the talk and debate, I was wit-
ness to an occurrence whose full significance I came to understand much later.

I was sitting in the editorial office of the magazine *Moskva*,
chatting with the woman editor in charge of the prose
section, when an elderly but still active and healthy-looking
man came into the room. He was wearing an expensive dinner jacket of black silk (the time was around midday) and
under his suit was a waistcoat of light beige, almost yellow
wool. All this, combined with his red tie, created a strange
impression. We were introduced, and I realized that I had
had the honor of meeting the satirist Arkadii Nikolayevich
Vasilyev.

I did not know then, of course, that I was breathing the
same air as the man who was to be an accuser at the trial of
Sinyavsky and Daniel. But I knew that Arkadii Vasilyev was
an unpleasant character, that he was one of the leaders of the
Union of Writers of the U.S.S.R., that he had not the slightest talent but did have more than his share of anti-Semitism.
But such qualities were common to many of the "hard-
boiled" Soviet writers, and I eyed this lively old man without
special interest.

But then Vasilyev raised the matter that had brought him

to the office—and I nearly shot out of my chair. It appeared that Arkadii Nikolayevich had come, as a disciplined member of the Party, to pay his membership dues to the Party organization of the *Moskva* magazine in whose books he was enrolled. The person who collected the dues was the woman editor with whom I had been talking. She joked about Vasilyev's being so punctual, opened his Party card, took out the record of contributions and asked him, "And how much do you have to pay this month, Arkadii Nikolayevich?"

Modestly and without any special emphasis he replied, "Three hundred and sixty."

Three hundred and sixty rubles! The woman editor's jaw dropped. Membership contributions are supposed to amount to 3 per cent of one's income, which meant that in the previous month Arkadii Vasilyev had "earned" 12,000 rubles (nominally $13,200). A skilled worker or a doctor in Russia will earn that amount in about ten years. The woman editor could not restrain herself. "Not bad, Arkadii Nikolayevich! You shouldn't be short of food this month. . . . "

The joke had a bad effect on Vasilyev. He looked suspiciously at me and with much displeasure at the woman editor and muttered, "It's nothing special. I've been paid for a scenario."

And with that he departed.

It was only later, when Vasilyev delivered his revolting speech at the trial of the two writers, that I understood for *what* scenario he had received such a generous advance on a scale unheard of in Russia.

The time is perhaps past when Russian poets will react to the unease of their times by acting out such extravagances of spirit as did Sergei Yesenin, once married to the American dancer, Isadora Duncan. This wild fellow, before his suicide, wrote a poem in his own blood. Today, protest takes a less melodramatic turn, but it continues.

Here is young poet Joseph Brodsky, on trial in Moscow for

"antisocial behavior," an official euphemism for ideas run counter to prescribed policy:

Judge: What is your profession?

Brodsky: Lyric poet. Translator.

Judge: Who has recognized you as a poet? Who has decided that you belong to the category of poets?

Brodsky: No one. Who decided that I am in the category of human beings?

Such direct answers resulted in an equally direct judgment. Brodsky was sentenced to several years in exile, to a chorus of underground and Western chagrin. But after two years, he was released.

The Brodsky case was in Khrushchev's time. Nikita Khrushchev was by no means liberal, but those who overthrew him in October, 1964, are even less so. Their grip on writers and the press as a whole has tightened a great deal. In 1966, those "progressive reformists," Brezhnev, Kosygin, and Suslov did not hesitate to sentence Sinyavsky and Daniel to seven and five years of hard labor respectively; in 1967, the young poet Victor Khaustov and the very young writer Vladimir Bukovsky were imprisoned for three years; in 1968, three intellectuals—Yuri Galanskov, Alexander Ginsburg, and Aleksei Dobrovolsky, after a shameful trial behind closed doors, were sentenced to seven, five and two years of hard labor respectively (the punishment imposed on Dobrovolsky was relatively "light" because he helped to prosecute the others). In April, 1968, the Soviet Party leaders introduced an extremely tough line toward freedom of expression; this tightening the screws was felt to be an obvious step back to Stalinism.

The Literature of Taboo

All over the Soviet Union, there are writers turning out stories that have no hope of official publication. Nevertheless, these works become generally familiar pursuing a devious route as they make their way from individual to individual around the country. Here is a brief version of one of them:

> After Stalin's death in 1953, the authorities began to release prisoners from the "corrective labor camps," and many of these camps were abolished.
>
> Deep in a forest, thirty miles from the nearest town, orders were received to break up just such a camp, and all necessary arrangements were immediately made. No specific orders, however, had been given to the man in charge of the camp's dogs. These were the Alsatians that had been trained to guard the column of prisoners as it marched to and from work.
>
> And that was how it happened that a dozen dogs, strong, fierce, silent, and trained to attack, remained behind as the only inhabitants of the empty camp. The last thing their guardian did was to throw open the door of their kennel to let them go where they pleased.
>
> The dogs first forced their way into what had been the kitchen of the deserted camp and gobbled up all the bones they could find. They also opened the garbage bins and ate everything that was to be eaten. Then, still hungry, they burrowed their way under the camp fence and disappeared into the forest. There they came across a wolf, which they pursued for a long time. They finally killed it and ate it without leaving a trace. Having satisfied their hunger, they lay down to sleep.
>
> The dogs awoke with the dawn and once again rushed off into the forest in search of food. Before they knew where they were, they found themselves racing down the main street of a town.
>
> It happened to be the morning of the First of May and, as in all the towns of the Soviet Union, the May Day demonstration was taking place. Columns of people, bearing above their heads portraits of their leaders, and banners with patriotic slogans, were marching down the main street and past the platform from which the local officials were viewing the parade. Everything was going on as in the Red Square in Moscow, only on a smaller scale.
>
> The dogs had been very well trained and had not yet had time to forget their training. When they saw the column of marching people, they immediately took up their usual positions along each side of the column, with equal distances between them. The local people were delighted with their escort,

though they could not make out how such powerful and beautiful hounds had suddenly appeared in a town where few people could afford to keep a cat.

"Just look at that!" said someone in the crowd. "The dogs are celebrating along with us. They're really just like people. They seem to understand everything. They are beautiful animals. Here, you—come here!"

But the dogs did not react in any way—they knew that they were not allowed to take any notice of whistles by prisoners, or to accept food from them.

Then one of the men marching in the parade noticed that his shoelace had come undone, so he stepped out of his column for a moment, moved to the side of the street, and bent over to adjust the lace. In a flash, without a sound, the dogs were upon him. Bearing him to the ground, they went for his throat.

Anyone living in today's Russia has no trouble seeing in those dogs the fierce bureaucrats of Stalin's time who have been able to hang onto their jobs into the less constrained atmosphere of today.

Here is another such parable.

I awoke and saw above me the sky of a summer morning. And a summer morning's sun and a summer morning's grass beneath my window. I ate a breakfast just like the morning: the yoke of an egg for the sun, spring onions for the grass, and black bread for the earth.

It took me twenty-seven minutes to reach the research institute where I worked, and nothing happened in those twenty-seven minutes worthy of note. But the guard at the door stopped me and said sternly: "Let me see your pass, sir."

That guard knew my face like the palm of his own hand and had never before asked to see my pass. But on this occasion, he took the document from me, and for a long time looked first at me, and then at the photograph, then back at me again. Finally, reluctantly, he handed the pass back to me and said: "Carry on, sir."

I entered the institute, and remembered that a new director was taking over that day and that I was supposed to introduce myself to him at once. The reason for the guard's unaccustomed caution then seemed clear.

Outside the director's waiting room was the same summer-morning grass and the same sunshine, and I caught myself thinking how nice it would be to jump through the window and lie down on that grass in the sun. And how nice it would be to feel the caress of long, slender fingers. Because those fingers that *did* caress me from time to time were rather shorter and rather fatter than I would have wished.

But I was summoned into the director's office. And no sooner was I in it than I noticed that everything had been radically changed. The director and his desk had been previously on the left; now they were on the right. The safe for important papers had formerly been on the right; now it was on the left.

The director rose to greet me and shook my hand with a kindly smile. He seemed as full of confidence as though he had been born in and had grown up in that very office.

"So you're a research graduate in physics and mathematics?" he asked condescendingly.

I sighed. "Yes, I'm still just a graduate. . . ."

"Now listen to me," said the director. "We have to reorganize all the work in your department. Radically. I think we shall have to start with the multiplication table."

I mentally thanked heaven that we had had the luck to acquire a new director with a sense of humor, and tried to react appropriately.

"Yes, that's the thing. Something like, say, two times two is seven, three threes are twelve, and five fives are thirty-three."

"You haven't quite got the idea," the director said without a smile. "I've got a few notes I've made here, which you can take as a guide and complete the calculations." He took a sheet of paper out of a drawer. "My notes say: twice two is twenty-two, three threes are a hundred and eighty, and five fives . . . . yes, five fives are one thousand eight hundred and twelve."

"Hm . . . ." I coughed, and then said cautiously; "But in actual fact three threes are still nine. . . ."

"What do you mean—'in actual fact'?" the director asked with a frown. "In this institute, they are going to be a hundred and eighty."

"But," I objected, my sense of humor draining away, "after all, if you take three apples and then another three, and then another three, you will have . . ."

"We are not talking about fruit and vegetables!" said my new boss sharply. "You can go into the details, if you like, but by and large it will be the way I've just explained it to you."

"Yes, but . . ." I said with sheeplike obstinacy, "if you take three tables and then three more, and then three more, you will after all have nine tables. *Nine!*"

"Not nine, but a hundred and eighty!" The director banged the palm of his hand down on the table. "What's the matter with you? Are you opposed to solving the furniture shortage?"

At that point I happened to glance into the mirror opposite me and saw that there were long, gray horns growing back out of my forehead. I suddenly wanted to drink, so I forced my sharp muzzle into the carafe on the table and started to lap up the water.

"Ne-e-e-e-xt please!" the director called out. But I could hear only the sound: "-E-e-e-e-e-."

I began to feel uncomfortable balancing on two legs, and it was with a sense of relief that I dropped to all fours. I rushed out into the waiting room, and with one leap I was through the window and out in the luscious grass. At that moment a flock of sheep was passing by and I joined them. For an image touched idly at my mind, something about caresses by long fingers. But it was too obscure, too elusive to grasp, so I dismissed it from my thoughts. I crossed over the wooden bridge and began to nibble at the grass like all the others.

One more example of a story from the "underground literature":

The aircraft rises smoothly from the runway of a Moscow airport and sets course for the town of Tyumen in the Urals. It is night and the passengers settle down more in their seats and soon doze off. The author alone finds it difficult to sleep. He is studying the odd positions of the sleeping passengers and the way their jaws hang down, the perspiration shows faintly on temples, the whites of eyes show through half-closed eyelids. He begins to think about the amazing happenings in this century, in which technology advances so quickly and people advance so slowly. People are exactly the same, not a scrap better than the people who lived in the Middle Ages, and you scarcely expect to find them sleeping peacefully at a height of 30,000 feet traveling at a speed of 500 miles an hour, as though they were riding in a stagecoach or in the compartment of an express train.

Suddenly someone shouts in a tone of authority: "Stop! Stop the aircraft!" Hello, what's this? How did this strange group of people standing at the entrance to the pilot's cabin get aboard? But there is no time for working this out, because the order has already been obeyed and the big jet airliner has already come to a standstill in midair, with its wings resting lightly on two clouds that have suddenly turned to rock. And one of the strangers, obviously their leader, says in a loud voice:

"Attention everybody! All passengers are to remain seated. We are going to check on your dreams. Citizens who have already registered their dreams with Aeroflot must produce their receipts. Those who did not register them will have to tell us the contents of their dreams. Is that clear? Very well, then we'll start."

The chief of the strange visitors looks very odd. And so do his subordinates. They are wearing long white stockings and shoes with large buckles—like French court shoes of the time of Louis XV. But what is particularly surprising is their faces, which are completely violet in color.

The strange beings go up to the front row of seats, where an apparently successful and well-fed citizen with a pink bald patch on his head is sitting. People like that are always provided with a piece of paper to cover every situation in life. And, sure enough, the citizen brings out his receipt, as pink as his bald patch, and shows it to the leader. Everything in order. The group of strange beings moves on.

A sense of alarm and impending disaster takes an ever stronger hold on the author. What is going to happen? Because he, the author, is not only without a receipt; he hasn't slept, and therefore he hasn't had any dreams. How is he going to prove that to the satisfaction of the intruders?

Meanwhile, there is something very strange happening up there in the front rows. A young man is refusing to describe his dream. "No, I've no receipt," he is saying to the leader, "and I have no intention of telling you what was in my dream. It is *my* dream, my personal property, can't you understand that?"

"I'll teach you whose property it is, young fellow," snarls the leader. "All right, take him off."

The young man is seized and stuffed into a sack. Puffing and blowing, two of the intruders drag the sack through the cabin toward the exit. They fling the door open, rush out onto the wing and hurl the sack, with its contents still protesting, onto the nearest cloud. When they have returned, their leader proceeds to deal with the next passenger.

This one stutters from fright. "I . . . I . . . Comrade chief, I have no receipt, but I will gladly tell you everything I saw in my dreams. Everything—everything!" And as he rushes through his story the leader starts to frown. "What is it, what's the matter, Comrade chief?" the passenger asks in alarm. "Have I really seen something wrong in my dream?"

"Of course you have seen something wrong!" the leader says sternly. "Or rather something that is not quite right."

"I admit my errors!" the passenger shouts desperately. "I confess. I was careless and I underestimated the danger. I swear that if you will pardon me this time and don't punish me, I will never, never again in all my life dream dreams like that one! Never!!"

The leader softens a little in his manner. "Since this is a first offense we shall not punish you this time. We are, after all, humane. We are fighting for man's good and for his happiness. We want man in our society to dream good, lovely dreams. We are in favor of realism in dreams!"

The chief of the visitors goes on for a long time talking in this vein. He talks for a whole hour. And at last the passengers applaud him with relief and pleasure.

But as soon as the visitors resume their checking of the passengers there is another unpleasant incident. Another passenger decides to resist. "I shan't tell you what was in my dream, so there," he shouts. "Who are you to poke your noses into my dreams? You are just people out of the past—just take a look at yourselves: old-fashioned clothes and faces the color of corpses. Your days are over, and we are no longer obliged to make our confessions to you!"

"Now there's a silly fool for you!" thinks the author. "He really is a fool."

The passengers do not even bother to wait for the visitors to take action: they seize the stupid fellow themselves, push him into a sack, and throw him out onto the cloud to keep the first

one company, saying "Let them lie out there together, the renegades!"

After this incident, the leader becomes quite good-tempered.
One of the passengers offers him some beer, and he sits down on
the arm of one of the seats and begins to chat with the passengers in a relaxed and friendly way. It seems as though he is no
longer interested in checking dreams. Everybody is satisfied and
flattered with the trust shown in them.

Suddenly the leader looks straight at the author and says,
"Listen, young man, I like the look of you. Would you like to
come and work for us? Then you'll be *our* man."

"But . . . I'm sorry, how can I . . . You see, I've already
got a job in Tyumen. I've got my wife there with me."

"Aw, come on, fellow, forget about your wife and Tyumen.
Do you realize who we are? We can do anything we please. If we
wish, we travel on the earth; if we want to, we can fly. When we
feel like it, we go round checking dreams, for example. And
do you know the sort of life we lead? We've all the money we
need, and all the nicest girls—not one of them ever refuses us!
And when it comes to holidays—we go only to the best resorts!"

Then, dropping his voice, he adds:

"And not just at home here, you know. We can go abroad as
well. The whole world is open to us—Nice, Naples, Rio . . . .
As for the color, they just take it for sunburn on the beaches."

"No!" says the author in a strained voice. "Do with me as
you please, but no. Not with you, not for anything!"

And with that he awakens. The plane is already coming in
to land.

There are hundreds of such stories floating about the Soviet Union, and the three I have chosen to use here are by no
means the most brilliant. They are merely typical, in that
they focus on the prevailing theme—personal freedom. The
absence of this is widely and keenly felt.

This kind of writing, now being produced by so many of
Russia's talented modern authors, should not actually be
called "underground" literature. The writers themselves
do not like that label, because it implies an activity that is
clandestine, furtive. They are usually quite open and direct

about their work, and are likely to seek every opportunity to have it published in the normal way.

Alexander Solzhenitsyn, for instance, the particular literary thorn in the side of the bureaucracy, has tried and failed to achieve publication of two of his novels. And theaters have been unable to secure official permission to produce his play *The Intellectual and the Camp Prostitute.*

The manuscript of Solzhenitsyn's new novel (actually his *first* novel) was returned to him by the editor of a magazine, with a note to the effect that the novel could not, alas, be published. The writer put the four big parcels containing copies of the manuscript into his case and prepared for the journey back to his home in Ryazan, some 115 miles from Moscow. But before setting off, he decided to do some shopping for his family. Weighed down by his heavy load and very tired—after many years in a prison camp his health is not good—Solzhenitsyn dropped in on one of his Moscow friends, with whom he left the case containing the manuscript, intending to pick it up the next time he was in Moscow.

That night, agents of the KGB called on Solzhenitsyn's friend and confiscated the novel. When he heard about this, Solzhenitsyn rushed immediately back to Moscow and demanded an interview at the KGB. They agreed, and, so the story goes, he told them that his friend was innocent and had no idea what was in the case. Solzhenitsyn added that if his novel constituted a criminal offense, they had better arrest him, since he was used to that sort of thing. And if it was not, they should return the manuscript to him at once, since it was *his.* The KGB were evidently very polite to him, explaining that they had taken the novel to prevent it from being passed around illegally. If he promised not to give it to anybody to read, he could have the novel back.

The KGB did in fact return it to him, and, as far as I know, Solzhenitsyn has kept his word and shown it to no one. In any case, up to my departure from the Soviet Union, none of my friends, people who never miss a single piece of writing, had laid hands on the novel. This is a great loss, because others—people working on magazines who have read the novel in the course of their work—have let it be known that it is a really shattering achievement. However, Solzhenitsyn is a writer of such great ability that nothing less is to be expected of him. A brave man, Solzhenitsyn not long ago issued a public statement, in which he denounced the withering hand of official censorship.

Not long before the well-known writer Vasili Grossman died, KGB agents burst into his apartment, searched it, and took away the second part of his novel *For a Good Cause,* which is a novel about the war. The authorities had refused to publish Grossman's novel, on the grounds that it was "ideologically uneven in quality," and the censor's department was worried lest it should begin to be passed round from hand to hand.

In this connection, one of the most powerful men in the Soviet Union is probably unknown to all but a handful of people in the West. He is General Michael Svetlichny, and his office is at number 4 Dzershinsky Street, Moscow. He is in charge of one of the divisions of the Committee for State Security. His is the Department of Literature and Art, and underneath all this official window dressing lurks the censor. Answerable to him are many bureaucrats of power and influence who are able to make the road to fame smooth or rough for any writer. Like appointed arbiters of literature in any country, such men have an official tendency to be extremely suspicious of honesty, directness, and real talent.

"I admire the perception shown by our critics," Vladimir Lakshin wrote in *Novy Mir* a few years ago. "It immediately picks on everything striking and progressive in our literature for the purpose of holding it up to condemnation and shame."

Such critics, in spiritual league with the censor, continue

to pump through the heart of Soviet literature the stale blood that goes under the name of "socialist realism." But such men, censors and critics alike, are now having an increasingly difficult time of it.

The censor's pencil, which sweeps with confidence along the lines of prose, boldly striking dangerous passages from short stories and novels, is often suspended helplessly over a line of poetry. The poor official, knowing that something is wrong, is faced with an unpleasant dilemma: either to ban the poem as a whole, or to permit it all to be published. And the censor knows there has been an unspoken agreement among poets over the last few years not to rewrite their verses according to official suggestions.

In Russia today there are, of course, poets who have handcuffed their muse to the Party line, and these men and women are widely published and greatly rewarded by the state. But they are of little consequence in terms of popular favor or honest critical regard. Of the poets who are of real importance—Yevtushenko and Andrei Voznesensky are probably the best known to the West—there is not a single one who has chosen to stand aside from the battle to speak and achieve the truth.

Poets who enjoy official favor may hold a reading in Moscow, and discover that they are reciting to large numbers of empty seats. But the scheduled appearance of Yevtushenko, Voznesensky, Bella Akhmadulina, or Boris Slutsky will pack a hall. The audience, brought to life by its favorites, will demand that these poets recite their verses again and again.

The result has been predictable. Official wisdom now dictates that poets should be "mixed" at the same recital. There will be the team of baying drones who recite the lyric Party line for most of the evening, and then, at the close, there will be the poet the audience has been patiently awaiting for so long. This one will often recite works that criticize the regime, although the criticism may be disguised in the cloak of an event of the last century. It may even concern itself with some tyranny of ancient Greece. But the audience understands immediately and applauds.

Interview with an Official Lion

In today's Russia, it is not only the writers who are conducting a kind of guerrilla war with the state. The conventions of belligerency are broad enough to include the other arts, as well. The nation's leaders, preoccupied with the need to impress upon all creative workers the special glories of "socialist realism," have expended their attentions on many of the other arts.

For instance, in 1962, Khrushchev visited a Moscow exhibit of modern art, and then hurried from the room before contamination could set in. His exit line was widely quoted: "Gentlemen, we are at war with you." On another occasion, gazing with no evident rapture at a piece of bronze statuary, sculptured in the modern manner, he was heard to promise that in the future, the government would be sure to find more practical uses for its bronze.

In that same year, the magazine *Molodaya Gvardia* asked me to interview the most prominent of Soviet artists, Vladimir Aleksandrovich Serov. In the world of painting he was, roughly, what Mikhail Sholokhov is in literature—a captive lion. I was attracted by the idea of seeing the animal in his own lair.

Serov had already given by telephone, his agreement to say a few words for *Molodaya Gvardia*. "I turn them all down," he rumbled in his warm, bass voice. "But I can't refuse the 'young guards.' I'm really very fond of that magazine. But you'll have to forgive me. I'll have to see you in my attic just as I am, without any fuss—I'm working at the moment."

Serov's "attic" turned out to be a magnificent studio on the top floor of a new block in the most beautiful part of

Moscow. Apart from the main room, which was enormous and could be divided into two sections by means of a sliding screen, there were other rooms. There was even a kitchen, despite the fact that Serov actually lived in another part of town. He turned out to be a short, round-faced man with gray hair, looking oddly like Khrushchev. He apologized for his appearance—the open-necked shirt and the trousers all rumpled and covered with paint—and invited me to sit down.

The first thing I noticed in the studio was a picture of gigantic size, which I had first seen in textbooks when I was at school. "Lenin Proclaiming That the Soviets Have Taken Power." It was supported on an incredibly complicated easel with all sorts of handles and levers.

"Vladimir Aleksandrovich," I said, "I didn't realize that that picture was still standing in your studio. Surely it was painted a long time ago? I remember it from my childhood."

Serov smiled at me in a kindly way.

"No, my dear boy, that's not quite the same picture as the one you remember. The original is in Peking, and this is a sort of author's copy, a rather more up-to-date version. Look more carefully at it and you'll understand."

I looked more carefully, and I understood. In the new version there was no sign of Stalin, who had appeared in the original, standing shoulder to shoulder with Lenin.

I asked him about another picture, rather smaller in size, also on an easel. This one, too, showed Lenin, here walking along a cobbled roadway accompanied by a crowd of typical workers.

"I am thinking of calling that 'Along With Lenin' " he said. "How does the title appeal to you?"

I approved of the title, while having some mental reservations about the picture itself. Like much official art, it was hardly more than palatable rubbish. I then left the uneasy subject of painting and asked Serov about his own life.

He said that he came from a small village on the road between Moscow and Leningrad. He was the son of a deacon in the local church, and he told me a few stories of the life of the clergy at the time of his childhood and youth, long before the Revolution.

Soon we were back to talking about art.

"Have you seen the daubings by Picasso at the French exhibition?" he asked me. "Not yet? Then I'll draw one for you."

He snatched up a fountain pen and quickly sketched a fairly accurate impression of Picasso's "Woman Under A Tree." As he drew, he made sulphurous comments about the various parts of the woman's body, and its color.

In similar verbal fashion, he ranged over the work of other foreign artists, some of them, like Picasso, devoted to the cause of Communism in their own countries. Renato Guttuso, the Italian, was one of these.

It was around this time that I asked Serov what he thought of the work being done by Russia's younger artists, and here his free-swinging tone took on the caution, the malice, and the suspicion of the high-ranking bureaucrat.

"Take this down word for word," he said. "It is most important that you should give my views with complete precision. It's like this: We have some very talented young artists who are working on important subjects and are continuing the best traditions of socialist realism. Apart from these, there are, unfortunately, quite a few so-called modern painters who bring discredit to our art with their daubing. There are even among the young ones some individuals who openly reject realism, speak in favor of abstract painting, and write goodness knows what. They must be given a stern rebuff. Do you know what these left-wingers get themselves up to? Only a few days ago there was a meeting to consider an exhibition of the work of nine artists. It was a bad exhibition, and the paintings were quite rightly criticized. One fellow went up on to the platform and said: 'From the point of view of socialist realism . . . ,' and there was a burst of booing from the hall. Then another started to say: 'As Comrade Khrushchev has pointed out . . . ,' and again there was booing. Do you see what I mean? I wouldn't be surprised if half the people there were agents of the FBI. They ought to be put in prison!

"I would have the hands of these so-called innovators chopped off so they should no longer be able to disgrace the walls of the galleries. . . ."

The position of the painter and sculptor today is little better than it was under Khrushchev. Even in the somewhat freer atmosphere of the moment, there are many artists who live in a state of tension, subjected to critical attacks and constant difficulties. In varying degrees, their creative capacity must still be directed toward the achievement of new triumphs of discretion—and even survival. When such men show their true colors in public, they are as likely as ever before to face official denunciation.

For example, in January, 1967, some young workers who were also lovers of art organized an exhibition of the work of eleven younger artists, including Oskar Rabin and Dmitri Plavinsky, at the club belonging to the Kompressor factory in Moscow. The exhibition remained open for exactly half an hour. Some people then burst into the hall and announced that it was to be closed down immediately, "because the premises are required for other purposes."

Although creative pressure is bubbling even more obviously under the veneer of Russian life, Soviet art has changed little, on its official surface, since 1962—the works of Serov are still held in high esteem, while men like Rabin and Plavinsky are still harassed.

But there is one especially interesting development to note here. The people who are interested in art are now beginning to turn away from the marshmallow sentimentality of the court painters and are demanding more real, more expressive art. It is no accident that the exhibition of the eleven young artists was opened in a workers' club. Art has always been a most powerful force, and it is making increasing headway, despite the censor.

Music on the March

People who deal in feelings on a mass basis can be very dangerous, which is the whole point of official nervousness about the Soviet writer and artist. In no area is this as obviously the case as in popular music. The Westerner who said he would rather write the nation's songs than write its laws was formulating a political axiom. What is at the heart of a really good song can often influence public policy. And I am not merely thinking of anything so obvious as "The Marseillaise."

There is no doubt in the mind of anyone in the Soviet Union today that its leading songwriter is Bulat Okudzhava. By any reasonable standard he is also the most popular singer in Russia. And yet, officially, he does not exist. Okudzhava was born in Moscow in 1924, and his father was liquidated during the purges of the 1930's. He wanted early in life to be a teacher, but soon switched his interests to the writing of poems, some of which were published. His war experiences impelled him to write a novel, but it was strikingly different from the war novels churned out by more obviously dutiful Soviet writers. Not only was his hero a realistically portrayed person, not manufactured from the customary heroic stencil, but his story lacked the conventional sentimentality of the "patriotic" novel. It was more direct and realistic. Naturally, it produced a certain amount of consternation. As Henrik Ibsen wrote somewhere, it is always dangerous to be right when everyone else is wrong.

Today, Okudzhava writes songs, singing them to his own guitar accompaniment. His songs are often about the war. Their tone is romantic or ironic, and they usually celebrate the kind of human themes that are not likely to be featured on a recruiting poster. He also writes love songs, and his music is melodious, his lyrics tender and rich with humanity. Because he speaks so directly to the heart, and sings out against the constraints that bind down the individual, it is easy to understand why he is considered a threat to those in power. And for this reason he is prohibited from recording his songs. However, they travel the length and breadth of the Soviet Union by the lips of those who love them, and by tape recordings.

Okudzhava was the forerunner of a kind of poetry aimed not merely at the intelligentsia or the especially literate, but at the millions. Now, others like him have appeared on the scene as writers and performers. The most talented have developed their own particular styles, and are helping to carry the genre of the "author's song" even further.

A song by another writer, Alexander Galich, called "Clouds," is a lament about the millions of people who suffered and were broken in Stalin's prison camps, and now, finally released, live out their empty lives on pensions. The singer of the song, receiving a pittance from the state, is now spending it on drink. He watches the clouds sail past him in the sky:

> The clouds float along, the clouds,
> To that distant land of Kolyma,
> And they don't need any lawyer,
> And they don't need any amnesty!
> And these days, just like me,
> Half the country sits in the bars,
> And in our memory, it's to that land
>   The clouds float, the clouds . . . .

Kolyma, of course, is the name of one of the more notorious labor camps.

Another of Galich's songs, with the ironic title "The Prospector's Waltz," pokes a needle through an important moral issue—the fact that millions of people, out of cowardice or out of concern for their own careers, remained silent while so much evil was being done around them.

> All of us have a little of the prospector in us,
> Because silence is golden.
> It's very easy to be among the rich,
> Very easy to be among the leaders,
> And oh so easy to be among the executioners—
> Just keep quiet, keep quiet, keep quiet.

One of the more recent of the "author's" songs to gain great popularity was a sharply satirical ballad of a teacher of Marxism-Leninism who is invited to inherit the wealth of his affluent aunt, who has just died abroad.

A sudden and marvelous change takes place in the personal philosophy of the teacher of Marxism. His Communist convictions evaporate, and he quits the institute and applies for a visa to the land where his late aunt's fortune awaits him. Meanwhile, all his friends and companions crowd around him, buying him drinks in the hope that he will later send them gifts from abroad.

Then, suddenly, a radio news bulletin tells of a revolution in that other country, one in which all private property has been taken over by the state. In his fury, our hero shakes his fist at the radio and shouts:

> How dare you, you scoundrels and layabouts,
> It all belongs to me and Aunt Kaleria!

That song, sarcastically enough, is named "A Ballad About Surplus Value," in honor of one of the central teachings of Karl Marx.

There are now in Russia many hundreds of such songs, all with the same general message. Like those of Okudzhava, they are usually circulated on tapes or by word of mouth. Most of them have simple tunes, quite easy to remember.

For a long time, the authorities pretended to take no notice of the songs, perhaps because they had no practical way of dealing with them. Okudzhava was of course dismissed from the staff of the literary journal on which he worked, and his poems were no longer published. For a while, he worked at a far more humble job in a small publishing house in Leningrad. But Okudzhava continues to write, play, and sing. (Recently, he was allowed to move back to Moscow and was permitted to visit France and West Germany.)

The custodians of Soviet ideology decided, in time, to tame the song writers with an official embrace. The newspapers began to flatter such minstrels, and clubs organized concerts at which the least offensive of the singers were encouraged to perform. But apparently no one cared to listen to such overly loyal troubadours, and the seats remained largely empty. When a few of the more potent singers were invited to perform, to help attract the crowd, the results proved disastrous for the authorities: they had unleashed a kind of whirlwind. An immediate damper was put on the entire program, and today silence prevails at the official level. Only down below, among the people, do the songs continue and spread.

Melodies Unheard

The men who make serious music in the Soviet Union have an easier time of it than their fellows in other artistic fields. The time is long past when Beethoven's symphonies and even Tchaikovsky's *Pathétique Symphony* might be banned. Gone are the days, too, when it was possible to accuse Shostakovich of formalism, that dread official curse.

Today, both classical and modern composers are performed quite freely in Russia. But even here, in the comparatively abstract field of serious music, one cannot speak of an absence of ideological control. Only recently, Shostakovich's *Thirteenth Symphony,* his newest, was banned after having been performed only twice. This was because it made the mistake of including Yevtushenko's poem "Babi Yar," and a musical passage based on a particularly stinging verse of that same poet:

> Czars, kings and emperors,
> Lords of all the earth,
> Kept their men in fear and trembling,
> But could never control mirth.

This sentiment was too dire a wound to the official bosom. Because the text could not be separated from the music, Shostakovich's symphony was banned in order to expunge Yevtushenko's words. The baby was thrown out with the bath water.

Stage and Screen

Voltaire wrote that the British like to shoot one of their admirals now and then, to encourage the others, and on this same principle, the men who make ideological policy in the Soviet theater like to do battle now and then with a particularly outspoken play. It helps, they feel, to intimidate the dramatists with some regularity.

Dimitri Tendryakov and Kamil Ikramov wrote a play called *The White Flag,* which dealt with a topic known to the West as "the war between the generations." The difference is that in the Soviet Union, this particular war represents a cleavage that runs with blood. On the one hand, the play portrayed the older generation, which had grown up under Stalin and had become accustomed to hypocrisy. On the other hand, there were the young men and women who search for the truth.

Thunder rent the air when this play was offered for production, and a special resolution of the Central Committee of the Komsomol was hurled at it. As a result, it never reached the footlights. At the height of this row, a friend of mine, a theater critic, offered me a more melancholy echo of Voltaire's comment about the British and their admirals. "This is nothing special," he said. "They are only carrying out Hitler's idea, that writers and artists have to have a finger wagged at them from time to time."

Since motion pictures are among the most obviously potent weapons of mass propaganda, it is only natural that the official hand should fall with special heaviness here. In the Soviet Union, there are fewer cinemas per thousand people than there are in any Western country. Tens of millions of peasants have no chance to visit permanent cinemas. From time to time, they are offered the services of "mobile cinemas" and can sit through whatever films are shown.

The average inhabitant of a Russian provincial town does not have a plethora of distractions and recreations to choose from, and this is the reason why even the lamest propaganda film will find some kind of an audience. The local movie house can get some people, even today, to endure yet another ponderous cinematic ode to socialist realism.

Yet, even with its trapped and tamed audience, the men who run Glavkinoprat, the organization that distributes films in Russia, were faced with a financial problem a few years ago. The country's movie houses were no longer producing the level of box-office profits that was expected of them. At this time, the gates were opened a bit, to permit the showing of French, Italian, American, and West German films. All of these are guaranteed money-makers in the Soviet Union.

But the purchasing commission that has the task of selecting the films to be brought in from the West must see that these imports are politically disinfected—they must not suffer from the "bourgeois ideology" of the outsider. Thus, some films of Fellini and Antonioni, for instance, have not been seen by Soviet audiences. The taboo is applied freely to most of the better films made in the West. The only ones considered untainted enough to be shown are those that have "progressive" themes. An American cowboy film in which the villain is the local banker is an example of the sort of import that arouses the greatest official pleasure.

It is an axiom of power that there is little point in being top dog in any society unless one can gnaw at the better bones, and the Soviet leaders are, of course, no exception to this rule. The Party leaders are very fond of Western films, even those, perhaps, in which the hero is a banker. They have projection rooms in their country houses, and there is a special group of people from Glavkinoprat who see that all the latest foreign films are delivered promptly to these private cinemas. The films are imported into the Soviet Union, ostensibly to be screened with a view to possible purchase. This procedure prevails even with films that are obviously a threat to the general Soviet mind. If the film is of any interest, a copy is made for the state film fund. This repository contains copies of every worth-while film ever made outside the Soviet Union, and they are available for showing to large numbers of people who make up the in-group of Soviet society today.

It would be unfair to dismiss all Soviet films as worthless propaganda, any more than it would be fair to damn all American films as worthless hymns to profit. Russia has many talented people making movies, and if they could be relieved of their ideological restraints, we would probably see many excellent films produced over there. Since leaving Russia, I have heard those who make Western movies complain in almost identical terms of their own constraints. If only they were relieved of the necessity to sell a maximum number of tickets, they say, what wonders they could contrive!

Even now, in spite of the difficulties under which they work, when almost every shot must be discussed endlessly to ensure its political correctness, there have been such noteworthy Soviet films as *Forty One, Ballad of a Soldier,* and *The Cranes Are Flying.*

"It's all right for the poets," said a cameraman friend one day with a sigh. "They can write a poem, pass it around to their friends, and the whole of Russia gets to know it in a week. But what can we do in the cinema? Just imagine trying to make an illegal film!"

A Last Look

Any honest view of the situation of the arts in Russia today would have to make the point that for large numbers of those who work in this field, there are only frowns and gestures of uncomprehending annoyance when someone from the West sympathizes with them about the shackles of official Soviet censorship. The sad fact is that many of them either see nothing wrong in such bonds, or are quite unaware of them. There is a more powerful inhibiting instrument at work among them—the censorship that such individuals impose on their own work, whether by conviction, or habit, or the wish to please the ringmaster.

In discussing such matters with men of the West, these Russians are likely to fall back on such trusty arguments as the censorship imposed on the artist in other countries by the demands of the marketplace. If a book, a painting, or a piece of serious music is aimed at only the very few, they will ask, then what chance has it of making its way in the market? Van Gogh and Mozart, for instance, did not do their suffering under Communism.

This argument is not as persuasive as some of those who use it would like to think. The men in the West who do not produce their works for money alone have usually been able, if they chose, to continue their work nevertheless.

What is especially interesting is that in the Soviet Union today, unlike in grimmer times, it is at least possible for even the officially rejected artist to continue creating along his own path. Throughout history, great artists have tended to be, if not renegades, at least to some extent at war with their times. This has been particularly true of the Russians. The pressure of nonofficial art continues to build, and a real explosion may yet be heard.

15

 ORPHANS IN PARADISE:
THE FARMERS

Those who work on the farms of the Soviet Union are, in a way, the special orphans of the Bolshevik Revolution, and this rural asylum comprises almost half the total population of the country. Great numbers of them live today, half a century after the event that was to free them from grinding poverty, under conditions not noticeably different from those from which they have been supposedly rescued.

Few informed people in Russia today would try to contradict the statement that the peasants are probably the most discontented single group living under Communism. It is not merely that the very nature of farm life is almost always hard, or even that it is especially hard under the Soviets. There is the additional affliction that the farmer tends to be, under any government, a conservative. Khrushchev, who had grown up in the Ukraine, Russia's breadbasket, understood this very well. "There will always be a psychological problem with the soul of the peasant," he said in 1962. "In the Soviet Union the farmer keeps going into his barn to look for his horses, even after they have been given to the collective."

The fact is that the average Russian farmer leads a mean life, and what is worse, he knows that it is mean. And he also knows that for him there is little likelihood of escape from it.

My Month in the Country

Some years ago, it was necessary for me to spend a whole month in the village of Danilovskoye, in the Kalinin region, not very far from Moscow. The experience was very instructive. The collective farm there is considered a good one, and its farmers are said to live well.

The village does, in fact, have many advantages when compared with thousands of other Russian villages. In the first place, it is only eight miles from the regional center, Kalinin, which has a population of 300,000. In the second place, it has a main road with a good stone surface, which leads to Kalinin, among other places. And in Danilovskoye there is electricity, while the office of the collective farm boasts a telephone. Both of these are blessings that are not available in roughly 60 per cent of Russia's villages today.

I could spend a long time running through all the things that this village does *not* have, such as a proper water supply, a decent drainage system, a shop, a medical center, or its own school. But the lack of these facilities is not something that the people who live there regard as a major problem. Here are some of the reasons why:

i. There are few exceptions to the rule that villages in Russia draw their water from wells, and that the villagers do not have toilets in their homes. The peasants have accustomed themselves from childhood to making use of the outdoor privy, even in winter, when the temperature dips way below zero.

ii. Kalinin, a large town, is only eight miles away, and one can get there easily enough to buy things, if only one has the money.

iii. In Kalinin, too, there is a good hospital, and if a man should fall seriously ill, the collective farm would transport him there by horse-drawn cart. When speed is important, the telephone in the farm office will get an ambulance to hurry from the hospital, which is only nine miles away.

iv. It is, of course, a pity that there is no school. But there is one in the village of Nekrasovo, only four miles away. The children of Danilovskoye make their way there and back, on foot, every day.

Incidentally, I have traveled a great deal by car along the roads of Russia, and have lost count of the number of school children to whom I have given a lift. You should know that a driver runs a great legal risk if he opens his door to an adult hitchhiker. For a first offense, the traffic police may fine you. For a second, you may wind up in court, on trial for "using a motor car for personal profit." It is usually difficult to convince the authorities that you gave somebody a lift out of mere kindness. But there is a tacit understanding between drivers and the police with regard to the hundreds of thousands of school children who have to make their way from village to village every day. No one is ever bothered for giving them lifts.

Unfortunately, there is very little traffic on the road leading from Danilovskoye to Nekrasovo—just an occasional truck. And even that is unlikely on such a road in midwinter. So the children have little hope of getting a ride. When they come onto the main road they stop and listen, just in case there may be the sound of a distant car or truck. But if there isn't, they set off on foot.

Actually, Danilovskoye ranks as a hamlet, not a village. This distinction is by now an anachronism. Before the Revolution, a village was distinguished from a hamlet by the fact that it had its own church. The distinction has remained, even though, with rare exceptions, the churches have long vanished from the villages. All that's left in Danilovskoye is the skeleton of a building that was once a stone church with a large dome. In the many years that have passed since it was closed, everything that could be stolen from it has been taken away. Even the metal covering of the dome has been removed, and there is nothing left but the bare framework. Apart from the church, there was once a wooden chapel by the roadside, but that has since been made into the village club. In the evenings, the young men get together there with the girls (of whom there are only a few left in Danilovskoye) and dance on the rickety floor boards to the sound of worn-out gramophone records. Sometimes there is a visit by a lecturer from Kalinin, and on such occasions the club is always full. The subject of the lecture is unimportant. In rural Russia, any form of entertainment will do!

There is one other place where people get together in Danilovskoye, and that is the café on the main street. It consists of a large wooden hut, dark-gray from age, in the gloomy interior of which stand a number of tables covered with pieces of oilcloth that has seen better days and nights. The café sells vodka, known as *suchok,* a locally prepared spirit of very poor quality, and, surprisingly enough, champagne. From time to time, there is a delivery of sugar, cheese, or tinned vegetables, all of which are snapped up almost immediately.

Not far from Danilovskoye, in the village of Mednoye, there is another café. In that one, everything is clean and well-arranged. There are attractive white tablecloths, and the waitresses almost sparkle in their well-laundered and starched aprons. There you have only to place your order and you are served quickly, not only with good strong tea, but even with a good hot meal. Why the difference? The reason is that Mednoye is on the main motor-road from Moscow to Leningrad—a good asphalt road that is used by foreign tourists. These tourists never turn down the narrow, cobbled road that leads past Danilovskoye, and this is why the local café bears no resemblance to the one in Mednoye.

I stayed in the village with an elderly collective farmer who enjoyed a relatively privileged position. For one thing, he was a member of the Party, and for another, he was chairman of the collective farm's audit commission. I did not know this when I was looking round for somewhere to stay. I simply chose the cottage that looked a little cleaner than the others. Even so, this cleanliness was only relative. The furniture in the one large room—the room that serves Russian peasants as bedroom, dining room, and living room—consisted of a long, homemade table, two benches, a few stools, and some trestle-beds for sleeping. Only I, the lodger, had sheets for his bed.

My hosts were exceptionally hospitable and friendly people. When they saw that I had arrived in a car, they immediately asked whether I would be making a trip to Moscow (about 140 miles away) in the course of my stay with them. When I said that I would, my host's wife, Anna Yefimovna, decided on the spot that she would not charge me for my lodging. Instead of asking for money, she asked me to bring a few things from Moscow—two kilos of smoked sausage, five kilos of sugar, and some yeast—"as much as possible."

"It would be wonderful if you could get a little flour, too," she said with a sigh. But her husband looked at her in amazement, and she waved her hand in a gesture of despair. "But I know you'll never find any."

It is a hard fact that flour is in short supply and is not on sale, even in Moscow. It is issued, at the rate of one kilogram per person, only on the eve of official holidays and at the New Year.

I did not ask the charming Anna Yefimovna why she needed yeast if there was no flour to be had, because I knew what she wanted it for. The most important religious festival of the year, Whitsun, was drawing near, and the yeast was needed for brewing homemade spirits. Whitsun was a more important occasion in Danilovskoye than Easter or Christmas. Traditionally, it was the village's own special festival. Although it has been thirty years, and even more, since the majority of the village churches were closed, the peasants continue to recognize and celebrate as best they can their own religious holy days. My host, a member of the Communist Party since before the last war, and an "activist" on the collective farm, was no exception.

A week before the Whitsun festival, I brought back from Moscow everything I had been asked to get, and a few bottles of good-quality vodka, besides. My host was so impressed that he made it a practice to bring me a jugful of milk every morning after that. As a local official, he had the right to buy it from the farm at an especially cheap price.

For four or five days before the actual holiday, Anna Yefimovna did not go off to work on the farm in the morning. When I came out onto the village street, I noticed that the other women were also busy in their own homes. This surprised me. I had often seen and heard the collective-farm brigadiers knocking on the cottage doors at sunrise, urging the farmers on to their work, cracking a joke here and dropping a swearword there. But on this occasion the brigadier in charge, old Misha, did not even knock on our door to call Anna Yefimovna. This could only mean that he had come to an understanding with her the day before.

I soon noticed something else out of the ordinary. A column of smoke was curling up from behind the little building that stood at the back of the cottage. This housed a sauna-type steam bath, similar to that used by most peasants, in a structure set apart from the house. I could see clouds of smoke rising from behind other bathhouses down the village street. Then at last I realized what was going on. The women were distilling liquor for the great day, and it was for this purpose that the farm officials had let them off from their work. Neither Anna Yefimovna nor the other housewives in the village turned out to labor in the collective until the feast day was over.

On Whitsunday itself, I was hauled out of bed earlier than usual, because the cottage had to be cleaned up. My host explored the family chest and brought out an attractive blue cotton shirt, which he put on. He also put on a pair of calf-leather boots that he had managed to save, since the war, for special occasions. His wife scrubbed the floor and the benches and laid the table. The first visitor to arrive, at noon, was her foreman, the same old Misha who had let the women off from work to prepare for the holiday. He was wearing a smart new suit and even a tie.

That day, Danilovskoye had to entertain many visitors from neighboring villages, and even from Kalinin. There was no icon, no remnant of the Russian Orthodox past, displayed in our cottage. After all, my host was a member of the Party. But occasionally Anna Yefimovna would mutter under her breath, and in some embarrassment, a prayer she had learned in her childhood.

The guests drank the homemade vodka out of large tumblers, grunted their approval, and praised the quality of the liquor. Between drinks, they made great inroads in the sausage and herring I had brought from the town, and in the salted cucumbers prepared by the host's wife. To me, the drink was thoroughly revolting. The smell of it alone was almost powerful enough to make me turn pale. Even the poor-quality vodka sold in the local café was immeasurably better, but no one was wealthy enough to pay the $3.00 or so that was the cost of slightly less than a pint.

Soon the whole village seemed to burst into life, and

people began to sing and dance. We could hear the sounds of several accordions being played, of girls screaming and men shouting. People moved freely from one house to the other, and everywhere they stopped they were offered a glass of something and a snack of whatever was on hand. My host also decided to make the rounds of the village, and he staggered back home, hopelessly drunk, toward sunset. Then he nearly collapsed at the gate, and when I managed to get him to the front porch, he said, "You—you want to know what you are? You're a lousy Jew—you're all of you a lot of damn abstaining Jewish bastards!" He added a few profoundly untranslatable remarks as I helped him into the house.

Several fights took place in the course of the evening, and the screams of women and the sound of breaking glass could be heard all over the village. "Sevka the tractor driver has been killed," Anna Yefimovna said as she came running in from the village. But to say he had been "killed" did not mean, in the language of the village, that he had lost his life. It simply meant that this Sevka had been thoroughly beaten up in a brawl, and that someone had stuck a knife or a piece of glass into his left arm. Or perhaps he had done it himself. It was just "among ourselves," as they say complacently in the village. The fight was stopped, Sevka's wound was bandaged, and no one bothered to call the police from town.

The celebration had been a great success. People went on talking about it in their houses and at their work for a week afterward. Stories about the Whitsun holiday, many of them imaginary and most of them humorous, began to spread. In the evenings, the storytellers, of which every village has more than one, would recite their own versions of some of the things that had happened at the village feast. And as the people of Danilovskoye listened, rolling with laughter at the frequently coarse jokes, they would forget for a few moments the dreary round of their labors, the scarcity of their joys, and the general severity of their lives.

Dreams and Realities

After the loss of the original revolutionary dream, which permitted the average peasant to hope that some day he might be a very prosperous fellow indeed, the dismal facts of the collective-farm economy have become like a dead weight in the rural Russian soul. There are no real incentives for the individual Russian farmer, and the low agricultural yield is one way in which it shows. Up to a short time ago, a farmer received wages only after certain other fiscal necessities of the farming operation had been taken care of. These included such things as debts, taxes, operating costs, and other considerations. One result of this was that a farmer was likely to get nothing at all in wages, unless he had the luck to be working on a particularly good collective farm. And a result of *that* was that only on such farms was there a stimulus for the peasant to work with any real sign of zest.

With the arrival on the scene of First Secretary Brezhnev and Premier Kosygin, a change was made. To improve the incentive among farmers generally, and thereby to increase production, wages were promised for *all*. Also, agricultural quotas were reduced, to bring them a bit closer to the realities of Soviet farm life. It is still too early to tell what this will bring about.

The Serpent in the Garden

An earlier attempt to step up the production of food has been flourishing with such generous abandon that each new success, paradoxically, results in a blacker eye for the philosophy of communal enterprise. This was the introduction of the idea of the personally administered "farm," or "kitchen garden." Each of these is, in effect, a private plot, which gets the personal attention of its owner-operator. On this patch of land, which averages about two-thirds of an acre, the peasant is permitted to maintain a cow and a few animals, and to raise vegetables or other worthy farm products. And, what is most important for him, perhaps, he is permitted to peddle the product of his private enterprise on the open market, and at prices that are not arbitrarily set by some official committee.

Russia is a large country, and these private plots represent, at most, only 3 per cent of the acreage under cultivation. Yet, despite its modest size in relation to the whole, the private Eden accounts for approximately one-third of all agricultural production.

The authorities are probably grateful for these booming results in a field that desperately needs some obvious successes. But it is not surprising that, as devout Marxists, they wince at every new victory achieved in their sinful dabbling with free enterprise. The spirit of the serpent of capitalism seems to flourish in these individual gardens.

16

 SOVIET SCIENCE:
OUT OF THE NIGHT

The people whom the leaders of the state fear most of all are
writers and artists. Because they deal in words and images,
they are regarded as the most likely carriers of ideological
infection. But a more subtle and yet more obvious danger
lurks in another quarter. The scientists are at least as
threatening to the regime.

A man of science, by the very nature of his work, has acquired the habit of subjecting any situation to logical analysis. In a way, he is like a man chasing a rabbit. He must
pursue the rabbit wherever it leads him. He is not able to tell
the rabbit that it must on no account stray too far from the

highway where the pursuer has parked his car. But through most of Soviet history, it has been the misfortune of Russian scientists that they were expected to deal exactly that way with the rabbit of scientific truth. If it happened to stray too far from the highway of "dialectical necessity," then the scientist was expected to turn away and address his attentions to some more tractable rabbit, one that could not be accused of the contaminations of "bourgeois science." Through much of that dismal time, the penalty for giving allegiance more to scientific truth than to political guidelines could be not only professional disgrace, but imprisonment and even death.

Today, the average Russian is proud of his scientists, of the men who sent Sputnik into space before the Western world could raise itself off the platform. They are proud of a science that has brought numerous Nobel awards to the men of their country. Only occasionally do they grumble over the fact that a country that can get a Gagarin to circle the earth in the time it takes to see a film cannot always get its building elevators to run properly.

Next to the political leaders, whose power is publicly acknowledged and just as publicly expressed, the most potent single body of men in the Soviet Union comprises the scientists. They constitute an elite group, especially esteemed and especially favored. As long as they keep their noses firmly to their test tubes, they may walk through their lives on a red carpet that stretches invitingly through years of honor and privilege. Russia's Academy of Science, for instance, is, outside of any political body, the single most influential group of men in the entire country. In American terms, it is the ultimate "think-tank." From it, the best scientific brains in the country set off on hundreds of different expeditions, all lavishly financed by a benign government (at least, benign for the moment), in search of answers to questions that puzzle fact-minded man. There are still certain limitations on the kind of rabbit such men may pursue, and in where they may permit the chase to lead them, but this cannot be compared with the iron strait jacket in which Soviet science was bound under Stalin.

There is a useful Western saying that maintains that "the boss's jokes are always funny." On the same principle, when one is living in a dictatorship, the boss's official pronouncements are always serious, even when one's private judgment shows them to be quite comic. To express the wrong reaction in the face of total power can mean the difference between life and death. The cemeteries of Nero's Rome were filled with the graves of men who wept when they should have smiled, and vice versa. Ultimate power grants the right, among many others, to be ultimately idiotic and to be taken seriously nevertheless. It may be, for all I know, that this is the real reason why so many men in history have tried to achieve it.

Hitler considered himself an artist—as did Nero—Mussolini was a novelist, Mao Tse-tung spent years pursuing the muse of poetry, and in 1909 Lenin, the chief architect of the Bolshevik Revolution, wrote a book on physics. He wrote it primarily to express the view that idealism had no place in science. Scientific concepts had meaning, he felt, only if they were anchored in the here and now of real existence. This was a personal point of view, of course, and not likely to be taken too seriously at the time that Lenin offered it. After all, he was expressing the view some eight years before he was in power. Once that power was achieved, however, the personal point of view took on some of the incontrovertible logic of the law of gravity.

For a long time, in the years that followed, scientific theories that were given some credence in the West were rejected out of hand, merely because they did not fulfill the expectations demanded of them by the official Soviet "line." It is not surprising that Sigmund Freud and his views were denounced as bourgeois infections. Psychoanalysis is occasionally given equally unfriendly treatment in non-Communist areas. But Albert Einstein, too, was for a long time blasted as an unmitigated lackey of bourgeois science. Stalin rose to the needs of this particular occasion by vilifying Einstein as one who had "succumbed to idealism and mysticism." In the catalog of Soviet scientific horrors, this charge is comparable to that of rape in an orphan asylum.

Science by Edict

On June 20, 1950, *Pravda* carried a statement from Joseph Stalin with which no sensible person can disagree: "It is generally recognized that no science can develop and flourish without a battle of opinions, without freedom of criticism."

The leader of Russian thought and action for almost three decades was letting the world know that he, too, was all for doing the right thing by science (and scientists), at least on paper. But the record, unfortunately, casts considerable doubt on the sincerity of this forthright opinion.

The nightmare that was cast over Soviet science in the name of Trofim D. Lysenko is not a new story to scholars. But for those to whom it is yet unfamiliar, it gives a particularly chilling answer to an old question: What happens when the needs of the scientist are made to yield to the needs of the state?

Lysenko, a Ukrainian plant breeder of no great professional attainments, first came to the attention of others in his field in 1929. He then made the claim that he had been able to alter the growth process of certain plant species by modifying their environment. His ideas were offered at a time of great agricultural crisis for the country, and the possibilities held out by his thesis were particularly attractive to the state's leaders, especially to those among them who knew least about certain fundamentals of modern science.

Gregor Mendel, the Bohemian monk, was the father of modern genetics, and it is from his brilliant work in the last century that we have derived the Mendelian laws that govern heredity. These laws maintain that from the very beginning of life, the reproductive cells are equipped with a tape, so to speak, that spells out the characteristics the organism is going to express in its life.

The laws of Mendel leave no room for the superstition that characteristics acquired in one's lifetime may be handed down to one's descendants. But Lysenko advanced just such a claim for his theories. His superiors, permitting ignorance and hope to triumph over knowledge and experience, quickly drew the young theorist to the official bosom. His ideas offered many fringe benefits at the time. Hitler had persuaded Germany of the wisdom of his own theory of Nordic supremacy; now Lysenko was holding out the attractive possibility that, in a generation or two, everyone in Russia could be a superman. In the briefest possible time, even the humblest Kurd or Mongol family might spawn a member of a master race.

Among geneticists, there is a story that underlines the folly of the primitive belief that characteristics acquired in one's lifetime can be passed on to one's descendants. It was often told by an American anthropologist, who would expose this fallacy to his college classes by pointing to the long history of the Jews. From their earliest times, he would observe, they had been in the habit of circumcising their males shortly after birth. Yet, despite this, each succeeding generation was required to perform this same service for its own males, and this had been the case for thousands of years. Leaning on Shakespeare for support, the anthropologist would then quote from Hamlet:

> and that should teach us
> There's a divinity that shapes our ends,
> Rough-hew them how we will.

For more than three decades, the science of biology in Russia was terrorized by the school of Lysenko. Those who shared the views of this school declared themselves to be the only representatives of dialectical materialism in the field of biology, and they had official sanction while they were about it. The country's leading scholars did their best to fight against this disastrous state of affairs, but Lysenko and his followers did not choose to meet the enemy in open scientific debate, preferring more practical means for enforcing their views.

For instance, in 1940, the prominent Russian botanist Nikolai Vavilov had the courage to tell Lysenko of his indignation at the illiterate and unscientific theories being advanced in the latter's name, and of the reprisals being taken against those who disagreed with them. At the time, many well-known professors were languishing in jail as a result of the political denunciations made by Lysenko and his group. Vavilov expressed the same objections to the Soviet Minister of Agriculture and in a short time, for his pains, he was seized and thrown into Saratov prison. The usual "authoritative commission" was formed to establish the nature and extent of his offense, and it concluded officially that he had sinned grievously. For one thing, it was charged, he had caused great damage to the airports of the Soviet Union. He had done this by recommending the sowing of the wrong kind of grass in such places. Vavilov died in prison early in 1943. He died ignorant of the fact that Britain's Royal Society had, during his imprisonment, elected him to honorary membership.

With the end of World War II, many people had the impression that life in Russia might now become more democratic, less inflexibly controlled from above. In the deceptively more relaxed postwar atmosphere, a number of especially courageous scientists again tried to demonstrate the futility of Lysenko's curious theories and the dangers that would result from their application. Leading the fight for truth at this time were two important members of the Academy, Pryanishnikov and Shmalgauzen.

Once more, Lysenko sought confirmation of his position from his official protector, Stalin. In 1948, a special discussion was arranged at the Academy of Agricultural Science. It turned into a kind of pogrom of those geneticists who had claim to genuine credentials. They were accused of being followers of such "bourgeois science fakers" as Thomas H. Morgan, Mendel, and August Weissmann.

Pryanishnikov had had the good sense or the good fortune to die three months before this discussion took place, so that the main thrust of Lysenko's argument fell on Shmalgauzen. As an aftermath of the clearing of the scientific air, some 3,000 persons were arrested, turned out of their universities, and deprived of all their academic degrees and titles. With this one blow, Lysenko was able to settle accounts with his more obvious opponents, and to keep them reasonably convinced of the official merit of his theories. At the very least, he convinced them of the wisdom of being discreet about any expression of their own theories.

Like Stalin, Khrushchev, too, had warmed the hopes and dreams of Lysenko, but in 1964, once Khrushchev had fallen, Lysenko was turned out to pasture as well. In 1965, while he was alive to read it, a Soviet journal printed a hilarious account of some of Lysenko's attempts to reverse the tide of modern genetics. For instance, he fed cream to calves, firmly expecting that this would increase the butterfat content of their milk, once they became cows. Failure. From pastry shops, he accumulated cocoa refuse, and fed this to cows, hoping here, too, for a higher butterfat yield. Failure. He imposed on Soviet agriculture the highly original view that when ordinary soil was mixed with manure on a fifty-fifty basis, the amount of the fertilizer was thereby doubled, with no depreciation in its quality. This break-through in agricultural thinking was especially welcome in some areas, because of the severe fertilizer shortage in Russia. Many farms, therefore, hastened to take advantage of this particular Lysenko theory. Again, failure.

The results of practically all Lysenko's theories and experiments tended to be consistent with the standard of achievement indicated here.

Other Fields, Other Terrors

The house of science has many mansions, and through most of them, crackpots have been permitted to wander, firing recklessly away at reputable scholars. All that has been necessary to justify such actions is that they be carried on under the banner of ideological rectitude. In cybernetics, in physics and chemistry, and even in the study of outer space, men committed to science have had to keep a wary eye for brickbats hurled through the air by the ignorant and the fanatical.

For example, all modern thermo-electric power stations are equipped with what are called single-pass boilers. It is generally known that this kind of boiler was invented in Russia. A small circle of specialists is aware that it was developed in the 1930's by an engineer named Leonid Ramzin. But even among specialists, few are aware that the single-pass boiler was created in Moscow's Special Prison Number 4. It was in that establishment, not at first sight the most appropriate for scientific research, that Leonid Ramzin and his colleagues (prisoners all) created the boiler that marked a major step forward in the science of energetics. It was an exceptional invention, so much so that Stalin gave orders for Ramzin to be released from prison and even decorated. It was true that the engineer died not long after, but for a brief time he was permitted to enjoy a measure of liberty and respect.

Just as exceptional, in its own way, was the special prison itself. The idea behind such jails was one of the more triumphant expressions of Stalin's creative powers. They were designed to harbor suspect scientists and more important engineers, permitting them to work at the more practical aspects of their separate callings, while denying them only such freedoms as are typical of the less practical interests of the spirit and the flesh.

The individual cells in which the inmates were confined were well heated and had proper beds with mattresses and even bedclothes. The prisoners were dressed in conventional suits and wore shirts and ties. Every morning, they were led out to work in the laboratories and designing rooms that had been constructed within the prison walls. Conversation was forbidden on all subjects not related to work projects. And the men were under the constant supervision of warders dressed in exactly the same way as the prisoners.

Once every two months, the inmates were allowed to have visits from relatives. These meetings were permitted not in the special prison, but in one of the general prisons, to which the men were transported on the rare visiting days in closed police vans. It was a violation of the sternest taboo for any prisoner to give a relative the slightest hint about where he was serving his sentence. The result of such a violation could be disastrous. Should a relative show up at the special prison, for instance, to inquire about a particular prisoner, he would be met with official ignorance: There were no prisoners there, he would be told. The man who had been asked about would then have eight years added to his sentence for betraying a state secret.

It was in such conditions that many specialists were obliged to put their brains to work to increase the strength and glory of the powers that had arrested them. And, as might be expected of scientists anywhere, they worked. Ramzin's boiler is only one evidence of how well they did their jobs. From just such circumstances came Sergei Korolyov's liquid-fuel jet engine for aircraft, Andrei Tupolev's TU-2 bomber, and quite a number of other equally useful products. In the case of Korolyov, the guardians of the state's scientific ramparts were thoughtful enough to take him to a nearby airport, so that he would be able to see how his engine worked. In this way, he was able to introduce improvements into the design.

Science was able to make headway for many years in this bizarre atmosphere. Great works were achieved not *because* of any special character in the Soviet atmosphere, but in spite of it. The man of ideas, perhaps more than other men, continues his work no matter what the circumstances. Copernicus, Darwin, Semmelweis and many others adorn the honor roll of those who have pursued the truth despite the official thunder. And there were those, of course, who were forced to continue their quest in the interior of the mind, their ideas walled in from the official view by silence and contemplation.

The Wheel Turns—Part Way

In 1965, the government of West Germany proposed to pass a law that would put an end to the prosecution of Nazi war criminals twenty years after the end of World War II. Speaking in defense of the proposal, the West German Minister of Justice, Ewald Bucher, explained that "We have to learn to live side by side with murderers." The next day, these words were reproduced in all Soviet newspapers, along with a stream of indignant commentaries.

At that time, while visiting one of the research institutes attached to the Academy of Science in Moscow, I was asked by a good friend, Doctor T., how I felt about the remark of the West German minister. It was highly unpleasant, I said.

"I am in complete agreement with you," said Doctor T., with a trace of irony in his voice. "But won't you agree, Comrade, that those Germans are lagging a long way behind us?"

"What do you mean?" I said.

"This is what I mean: They have still to learn how to live side by side with murderers, whereas we Soviet scientists learned how to do it ages ago. Take me, for example—in half an hour I'm going to lunch in the academicians' dining room, where I'm bound to meet our old friend Lysenko. There are a dozen like him in our blessed institute, and plenty of them in the other institutes as well."

The German statement had apparently opened many old wounds, and Dr. T. told me there had been much private discussion of it among his own more trusted colleagues.

Let the reader not mistake me—I, too, was in the Soviet Union during the period when Lysenko's word constituted biological law. As a science writer, if I had been commissioned to write an article on biology, I, too, would have hewed to the master-farmer's line. To do anything else would have been nothing less than an act of suicide. The author of such a piece of independent thinking would have been put away in a prison camp or shot, and not a living soul would ever have known what he had done.

I did not cry the praises of Lysenko, comparing him with Newton and Archimedes, only because fortune had spared me this particular disaster. Prior to 1947, I did not write on science topics, and from that year to 1953, all my time was spent in a prison camp. When I was released, on the death of Stalin, the pressure to sing the brilliance of Lysenko had somewhat diminished. If it had not, then in all probability I, too, would have been forced to join the angels' choir.

There have been voices here and there that have spoken out to some degree against what the cold hand of ideological necessity has done to the scientific spirit. But until recently, only the very greatest names have dared to do so, such as, for instance, world-famed physicist Peter Kapitsa. Men like him, of rare eminence in their specialized fields, were occasionally able to dare more. I do not wish to detract in the smallest degree from their courage, because equally famous men kept their silence. But the fact of their eminence and even indispensability provided such as Kapitsa with a thin measure of immunity denied to lesser mortals.

Most men in the sciences bowed their heads to the whirlwind. They tried to keep their attentions fixed to their work, compromising only where absolutely necessary, giving ground only where the categorical imperative of survival—not to be underestimated in any society—dictated the terms of that survival.

And what of Lysenko himself?

Though deposed, he was never actually punished for inspiring his reign of terror in the sciences. In fact, there is no question of any investigation taking place. The Central Committee of the Party has now imposed a ban on the publication of any material exposing such as Lysenko. As a scientific journalist, I have attended briefing sessions at which we were warned not to excite passions, because this might lead to a return to the very same methods that were used by Lysenko and his followers. We must not be inspired, we were told, by a spirit of mean revenge. It was our duty, rather, to ensure that there was freedom of opinion in the world of biology.

This unusually generous and high-principled attitude can be very easily explained. Lysenko's associates, the same people who were so quick to destroy honest scientists on his instructions, are still entrenched in the Central Committee of the Party. They can scarcely be expected to permit anything like an objective investigation into their own past actions. To paraphrase, in a way, a remark of Winston Churchill, they have not achieved power merely to preside over the liquidation of their own private empires.

Rumblings on the Frontier

In the somewhat relaxed official attitude of today, the scientist is beginning to poke his head up from his work, where years of terror had encouraged him to keep it buried.

In many quarters, he sees obvious inefficiencies in the way the machine of Soviet society is functioning. And like the man of science anywhere, he likes to believe, in many cases, that he knows exactly how it may be fixed. And that is why the Russian scientist today is at least as dangerous as the writer or the artist.

One thing that particularly bothers him is the plague of bureaucratic planning. In all research institutes and laboratories, both secret and otherwise, a great deal of time is spent drawing up all sorts of plans, projects, and descriptions of future scientific themes. This mountain of paper has to be produced in order to obtain the necessary funds to carry on with one's work. It must be remembered that Parkinson's laws are no respecters of national boundaries. A highly placed bureaucrat in charge of a particular branch of scientific activity must be persuaded by what he finds in a particular paper that his approval is being sought for something worthwhile, a project that will in time yield a noticeable return for the nation's economy. Only when he is so persuaded is he likely to give official clearance to proceed. When it comes to projects that are highly theoretical or abstract, those that promise no immediate return, then the scientist must use all his ingenuity—and paper—to make his appeal especially persuasive. If Albert Einstein had been a scientist working under such conditions, it is quite likely that his request for funds to implement his study of a theory of relativity would have been thrown back in his face.

At the crucial desk there is often some virtuoso of the rubber stamp to read and evaluate with bureaucratic suspicion, and this condition produces, now and again, a measure of scientific disorder. What this has brought about in the new, partial dawn of Soviet science, I can touch upon with a personal experience.

Some 2,500 miles from Moscow, on the bank of a deep Siberian river, surrounded by gigantic pines, larch, fir, and cedars, there is a beautiful town that has been in existence for more than twenty years, but that is not marked on any map. It does not have a name, only a number, and if you should wish to send a letter to someone living there, you would have to address it to one of the larger Siberian cities, adding that special number. The people who live in this secret town have given it, among themselves, the name of "Kitezh." This is a name borrowed from Russian folklore, where it describes a town cut off from the rest of the world by an impenetrable bog.

I spent several hours in that secret Siberian town, from midday to nine in the evening. It was not a long time, but enough to make the experience the most striking of my entire life.

Aside from a handful of the very highest statesmen and a few scientists from Moscow who are directly involved with the supersecret work going on at "Kitezh," nobody is permitted access to this town. It is probably a matter of great chagrin to those responsible for maintaining secrecy that the town's essential inhabitants require certain human services: They must have food and drink, houses to live in and vehicles to move about in, and even, on occasion, some means of diverting themselves. For such reasons, there are a large number of residents in the town who are not concerned with its secret work, but who serve rather to ease the flow of life for those who are so concerned. This serving group is thoroughly reliable, of course, having been well screened for loyalty, but it is composed of human beings. And in their travels back and forth between the large Siberian city with a name and the secret town with a number, normal frailty has permitted just about everyone in that city to know of the existence of the town, and even a few other things about it as well.

Perhaps it is for this reason that foreign tourists who travel through Siberia are not permitted to drive through or even fly over that large city. It is true that trains carrying foreigners are permitted to stop at the station there, but every care is taken to see that foreign passengers do not leave the station building or have contact with unlicensed personnel.

In Moscow, I had heard a good deal from scientists about the existence of a mysterious town in the forests. The most incredible stories were going around: That the shops there displayed everything that could be found in Paris or New York and sold them at giveaway prices; and (a story to scorch the Russian heart with envy) that there was not a single "communal" apartment in the whole city—each family had its own apartment; and that (equally fantastic) the scientists who worked there and happened to be Party members were *not* obliged to attend Party meetings. Being somewhat skeptical by nature, I was not inclined to believe all the extraordinary things I heard about this Siberian town. But I was highly curious about it, nevertheless.

I must not explain how I succeeded in achieving my aim of visiting "Kitezh," even for that brief span of time. To do so might endanger the lives of many people. I might add that in their conversations with me, none of the scientists dropped the slightest hint about their work, and I asked no questions about it. In the course of my visit, I was interested only in human beings, and in what they were thinking.

It is part of the local mythology that Khrushchev himself visited the town on one occasion, and boasted that he had not come across such a place "even in America." I had not been to America, so that particular image was lost on me, but it is instantly apparent to a Russian that "Kitezh" is much different from other Soviet towns. For one thing, it is immediately obvious that its inhabitants are well off. Also, one senses there a kind of tranquillity, an atmosphere of urban ease that is not to be found elsewhere in Russia. The town is well planned and well built and there are no queues in its shops, which is enough to raise the eyebrows of most citizens.

By comparison, the more recently opened scientific center near Novosibirsk, which is not cut off from the rest of the world by official secrecy, is a completely Soviet town. It is distinctly different in appearance from this "Kitezh."

To finish with the more obvious features, it was not true, I discovered, that there were fantastic shops with their goods on sale for almost nothing. But the selection of goods was certainly far greater than what could be found in the best department stores of Moscow. There were also a great many imported articles on sale, and one could buy a motor car (Soviet, of course) without having to wait a long time for it. In Moscow, awaiting delivery of the same model, you would have to sit around for four or five years. But prices were no different from those elsewhere in the Soviet Union—unreasonably high.

The very considerable difference in the standard of living of the people here was plainly due to the enormous salaries that were received not only by the scientists, but by the other employees as well. It was apparent that this form of voluntary imprisonment in the secret town was well paid, though I did not care to enquire exactly how much they received.

Armed with an introduction from a young professor in Moscow, I called on one of his friends who worked in "Kitezh." My host welcomed me with exceptional warmth, picked up the telephone almost immediately, and began to round up some friends for a talk. Within half an hour there were nine people assembled in the room with us. The room, by the way, was fitted with Hungarian polished furniture, and expensive rugs from Azerbaijan carpeted the floor. On the table was a bottle of Cuban rum and a jar of lemonade, and as the talk progressed, each of us helped himself at will. Some hours after the conversation was at full speed, my host's wife brought in a large tray of cold snacks. We ate as we talked, "so as not to waste time from our real nourishment," the host said.

I was completely absorbed in the conversation, and was awakened to reality only when the telephone rang. Someone was calling to tell me that a car was on its way to fetch me, because it was time to return to the city. It seemed to me like returning from a fairy-tale world to one of mud, noise, and statistics.

But let me return to the beginning of the conversation. While the other guests were arriving, my host and I were feeling each other out, as it were, for subjects we might talk about. As frequently happens in the Russia of the present day, we began by talking of the latest events in the literary world, where the most provocative item at the moment was the appearance of Solzhenitsyn's prison-camp story, *One Day in the Life of Ivan Denisovich*. Then I recited a few underground poems, which were received with considerable enthusiasm. When I was asked to give the names of the authors of the poems, I hesitated and gave an evasive reply. At this, my host frowned.

"You came to us with a first-class introduction," he said, "and you'll soon see how much you're trusted here. But please, we'd like this to be a mutual trust. I can assure you that there are only *real* people present in this room. And you can trust the walls too—they're completely reliable and have no ears—we check them personally every week, by scientific means. So—please trust us!"

This appeal was presented in such a way that all my doubts, all my ordinary caution immediately disappeared. I started to talk with the fullest candor, a good deal more openly than I might have dared even in my own apartment back in Moscow. In my apartment, after all, I had neither the equipment nor the ability to check the relative friendliness of the walls.

Very soon, the conversation turned from literature to politics, and from then on I no longer talked but simply listened. I will recount here only the main ideas that were discussed, to keep from being entrapped in details. Of course, I took the important precaution of not writing down any notes of the conversation.

These men, dealing professionally with facts, tended to be bothered, even appalled, by the obvious waste, illogic, and disorder that they noted in "the way things are." If the existing political and economic system was to function properly, they thought, there was much repair work to be done. Their criticism went beyond the customary humanitarian objections to the manifest cruelties of the regime. The time had come, they said, to apply some intelligent scientific analysis to the status quo. If a rational program could be worked out for such an analysis, more or less discreetly, then it might be possible to produce certain changes in the economic and political situation that would permit the Russian machine to work far more smoothly.

To put the situation in its loosest terms, they were like guests trapped in a hotel room in the country, during a rainy weekend. The radio in the room is bad, rising and falling wildly at times, the dial functions only enough to produce exasperation, and certain choice local stations are not receivable. Each of the guests is a radio engineer, yet each is under absolute instructions not to improve reception by tinkering with the set. And there is a notice on the wall of the hotel room, informing them that the set has been officially approved as the best that modern science has to offer—anyone who says otherwise will be put in jail, and perhaps even shot.

It was the conclusion of the scientists I listened to that the system must be changed and brought to a qualitatively new state. In that new state, they felt, both political and economic self-adjustment should be possible, with changes and advances to be made on the basis of scientific good sense, backed by the will of the people and the operations of the market place. For too long, these men felt, dictatorship had per-

mitted bureaucratic whim and ideological caprice to dominate policy in the economic and political fields.

These men were not talking about the kind of revolution
that would lead to sudden strife, resulting in chaos, blood-
shed, and death. They were all quite aware that Russia had
already suffered enough in this century from revolution,
famine, and war.

The kind of change they envisioned could not be achieved
overnight. Before the machine that is the Communist state
could be persuaded to permit a retooling for more realistic
operations, a transitional stage would be necessary, a period
in which the country would be governed on the basis of
directly scientific decision. Whenever that last phrase is used,
the word "technocracy" rears its head, and Soviet propaganda
has worked overtime to throw mud at this word. But technocracy is likely to be no better and no worse than the men
who administer it, which is perhaps as much as can be said
for either "Communism" or even "the free world."

The immediate course, then, as these men saw it, was to
get as many of their kind—scientists who thought as they did
—into positions where decisions are customarily made. The
situation was favorable for that approach, because the masters
in the citadel are always on the lookout for new and talented
recruits to man the desks where decisions are made. But
there were obstacles. To take such a position imposed the
taking of what amounted to an oath of loyalty to the system
"as is." Many scholars have found this personally difficult to
do. They cannot swallow such a bone, and have thereby cut
themselves off from the possibility of being appointed to
senior administrative posts. Also, like true scientists in any
country, they consider the business of administration to be
incompatible with serious professional work.

But right there in that secret town, there were scientists
who had been convinced, because of the larger objective, to
take on administrative tasks. Of the nine people present in

the room with me, seven were members of the Party, and the Party organization in the town, I was informed, was growing steadily from the influx of those who had seen the new light.

The men I listened to are wise enough to realize that the road they have chosen is not an express highway. It is more like a precarious path over mountains and through jungles. They know that much will depend on the support or opposition offered by other sections of society. "You are the first journalist we have ever met," one of them said to me, "and what's more, you work in the field of popular science. It's a very important thing for us."

It was crucial, they felt, that writers, and the press, should be persuaded somehow to inspire confidence in the scientist's special ability to make an objective judgment about facts, his internationalism, and his relative freedom from dogma. They were well aware that even among scientists there existed, as they put it, "careerists, cowards, and plain rogues" (unhappy shrugs of the shoulders here), but the struggle would continue nevertheless. One important point they made was that major scientists were going to write more often and more freely for newspapers and magazines, and were going to make themselves available more often for interviews. Their opinions were no longer to be limited to narrowly professional matters, but would include views on questions that affected the future of mankind. They felt that when a member of the Academy speaks, people usually listen; also, they felt, the censor is not as inclined to cut out a scientist's less orthodox remarks, out of respect for his eminence.

It is important to make the point that this is not a conspiracy, not a new party setting out to seize power. Current authority might arrest truckloads of people such as those I listened to, but the movement would continue. This is because it is a movement that operates without a leadership. What is determining policy here is the sense of like-thinking members of the scientific community. This policy is dictated more than anything else by a generalized yearning for more obvious efficiency. To understand its main lines, no scientist requires direction from above. Each man operates as an infiltrator within the apparatus of the Soviet society. He is, in effect, an individual evangelist, who spreads a gospel identical to that offered by a growing number of other such evangelists: that the country can be made to function far more intelligently.

At this stage, it is hard to tell how long it will take to achieve the dream of the men who spoke to me. It is harder still to predict that it will ever come about. But it was made clear to me that, at long last, a step toward the light was being taken. A small step, perhaps, but an important one.

There is a profound discontent over the Party's meddling in professional affairs. The iron hand of bureaucratic control has become more relaxed in the past few years, but even so, the philosophy of "dialectical materialism" continues to mark many of the paths that may be traveled in the laboratory. And far too many worth-while activities are rubberstamped "off Limits," because they do not serve the narrow purposes of the regime. Also, the scars of the terror and persecution of not so long ago are still too fresh to be forgotten.

That, very briefly, is the burden of the story I picked up from those about me in the room at "Kitezh." In time, perhaps, the fog will begin to lift, and the special rays I felt in that room will make themselves felt throughout Russia.

In January, 1968, four persons, intellectuals all, went on trial in a Moscow courtroom for "anti-Soviet activity." A petition was presented at the time, asking for "full public airing" of the trial in the press, as well as an impartial selection of witnesses for the defense. The petition was signed by thirty-one writers and scientists. Such a gesture would have been unthinkable only a short time ago. It, too, is a sign.

Three centuries ago, Galileo pointed out that the earth

actually moved. He was told to shut up, because his view was upsetting to those about him who held absolute power. He agreed to keep quiet, although legend tells us that as he agreed he murmured under his breath, "But still it moves."

Perhaps Soviet scientists are on the way to proving to those presently in power in their country that the earth actually moves.

17

 STRANGERS
AND OTHERS

The Russian people have a great deal of interest in foreigners. A stranger among them, from an obviously foreign land, is likely to be asked almost immediately what country he is from. This special curiosity is to be expected, perhaps, from a people who have been immobilized within their own borders. The average Russian who wishes to look at another part of the world is able to do so only through the special lenses provided by the government's official prejudices. It is not easy for him to get a view of France or the French, for instance, that does not have the Kremlin stamp of approval on it. Consequently, there is a great eagerness to know all about foreigners, when one of them comes into personal view.

Unlike relatively homogeneous countries, where most citizens derive from approximately the same stock, Russia has a population that is dazzling in its variousness. In this respect, it is like the United States, another country in which people of a wide variety of languages, colors, and ethnic backgrounds move about under the same family name—Americans. The situation is not as bewildering today as it was in 1934, when the Soviet Government found it necessary to print schoolbooks in no less than 104 separate languages, each one of them native to some part of the country. But the great multiplicity of separate peoples remains.

Very few people among the 235 million who inhabit the Soviet Union can boast that they have really traveled the length and breadth of their country. More than half the citizens of the Soviet Union die without ever having been to Moscow. About the same percentage spend their whole lives in the European part of the country without ever setting eyes on the Urals, Siberia, the Far East, the Far North, or Central Asia. Traveling is expensive and beset with difficulties, so that no one travels unless it is absolutely necessary. And those who have the means to take a summer holiday are mostly inclined to make for the warmth of the Black Sea, casting only a fleeting glance at the strip of Russia visible from the train or airplane. It is this lack of contact with other parts of Russia that makes for a kind of coolness on the part of one Russian when he deals with another whose background is obviously different from his own.

But a foreigner is not a member of the very diverse Russian family. He is a true exotic, a visitor from a far country who will be here today and will then disappear. He represents a chance to know something about that mysterious world beyond the border, about which one hears mainly through official bulletins.

In recent years, this curiosity has been increased by the reports of Russian travelers who have been permitted to visit other countries. The tales they have brought back of the ways of life and thought in other parts of the world have whetted the Russian appetite for information about other peoples. They are particularly interested in hearing everything they can about America and the Americans, and despite the fact that government propaganda presents an unsettling picture of American nefariousness and corruption, the sickness of American life under rampant capitalism, and the earth-shattering violences of American foreign policy, it is the American, more than any other foreign nationality, that the Russian is most attracted to and most eager to know about. It is only a minor paradox that the average Russian shares his government's concern about America's capacity for evil, and yet continues to feel attracted to Americans as a people.

Lately, however, there have been some disturbing blemishes appearing on the official record in Russia. In recent years, African students who have come to the Soviet Union on scholarships, have brought with them the ingredients of a social problem. Many of these students, incidentally, have come to Moscow's Patrice Lumumba University, named for the martyred Congolese leader.

Russian girls who have accepted dates with Africans have been harassed by white students, and an atmosphere of mutual bitterness has naturally ensued. In the winter of 1963, one of the African students was found dead under mysterious circumstances. The Russian version of the facts held that he had been drinking a great deal, had fallen from a train, and had died of exposure in the desperately cold weather. But his friends had a somewhat different story. He had been dating a Russian girl, they claimed, and because of this he had been beaten to death.

Like good radicals, the Negro students carried their grievance into the streets, demonstrating in Red Square, no less. They displayed banners that demanded justice. But they got little sympathy from the government, which chose instead to hush up the situation.

That single incident was only the most dramatic. There have been others that lead to the unmistakable conclusion that the government policy of opening its arms to African students to promote good feeling, has excited ill will instead.

For instance, as I write this, I have before me a copy of the *Daily Telegraph,* of Lagos, Nigeria, dated May 20, 1965. This, you must remember, is quite some time after the death of the African student at Lumumba University. Here is the first paragraph of a dramatically headlined news story:

> The Russians are again looking for someone to blame for their own problems. A few weeks ago twenty-nine Kenya students, after a long hunger strike, returned to Nairobi. They could no longer stand the Soviet oppression in the city of Baku. In March a Ghanaian student was murdered in that city and the Soviet police promised to investigate. No one has been arrested for this awful crime.

Some more quotes from the same news story:

> Now more students from Kenya, Nigeria and Ghana (and maybe other countries . . .) are asking to be sent home. Students who have left complain of racial discrimination. They are ignored in most restaurants and they are beaten when a Russian girl makes friends with "one of those strange Africans." . . .

The article ends on this familiar note:

> The Russians are now trying to put every African in Moscow on trial. They want to control the African like they control the thoughts and movements of their own citizens. In short, the Russians are trying to pressure our students to stop seeing others from the West. It is a policy that can not succeed.

By 1967, more than 1,000 African students had left Communist countries to continue their studies in West Germany.

Friends and Neighbors

As I have noted earlier, the average Russian is, on the whole, on generally good terms with those who share with him the honors and burdens of being a Soviet citizen. But things are not quite as good in this area as his government frequently tells him they are.

Here is an extract from a speech made by the Soviet writer Grigory Svirsky, a member of the Communist Party, at a meeting of Moscow writers in the spring of 1966:

Last summer I went on a trip around the Soviet Union with a group of friends. One day we arrived in Ossetia and put up our tent on the outskirts of a little mountain village. A group of local inhabitants approached us, and within a minute we had all—according to the rules of Caucasian hospitality—been invited to a wedding that was just about to begin in the village.

The invitation was accepted with great pleasure. But just as we were ready to move off, one of the local people eyed me very attentively and then said suddenly that I would be well advised not to go to the wedding. Nobody understood what the reason might be, but I shrugged my shoulders and remained in the tent.

Soon I noticed some people running in my direction. While they were still far away they started to make beckoning gestures. The group included the village elders and the same young fellow who had advised me not to go. They fell all over each other to apologize to me, and practically carried me to the banqueting table. "Please forgive us, dear friend, for making such a terrible mistake!" one of them explained. "You see, we took you at first for a Georgian."

We later continued our journey through Georgia. As I was walking down a street of the Georgian capital, Tiflis, a couple of young drunks came up to me and asked me something in their own language. I replied in Russian that I could not understand them, with the result that the one who had asked me the question punched me in the face.

This incident brought us to a police station. When the officer on duty looked at my identity card, so he could get the name of the victim for his report, one of my attackers glanced into it and was obviously shaken by what he saw. "Oh, please forgive me," he said. "Do what you like with me. You see, we took you for an Armenian!"

Then we visited Estonia, and there nobody wanted to talk to us at all, because the Estonians regarded me as a Russian. And when our journey was over and I had returned to Moscow, I discovered that I had lost my job as a member of the editorial staff of the magazine *Friendship of the Peoples,* because I am a Jew. So what about the friendship of the peoples in our country, Comrades?

Svirsky had the courage to raise what is in fact the most strictly forbidden of all subjects in Russia, the question of the real relationship existing among the various nations in the country. And he not only did it in public, but in the presence of the Party's chief ideologist. The Secretary of the Central Committee of the CPSU, Comrade Pytor Demichev, was in attendance at the meeting.

Times have certainly changed. In 1947, I spoke about anti-Semitism in the U.S.S.R. with a fellow student. He informed on me to the secret police and, within a few days, I was on my way to the prison camps for seven years. But Svirsky talked about the same subject to a large audience, part of it official, and he is still, as far as I know, at liberty. Undeniably, this represents progress.

When Nikita Khrushchev condemned Stalin from the platforms of the Twentieth and Twenty-Second Congresses of the CPSU, he talked about the prisons, the tortures, and the executions. But there was one subject that he practically ignored altogether, and that was Stalin's "nationalities policy" and the crimes committed because of it. The Kalmuks, the Chechens, the Ingushi, and the Crimean Tatars, for instance, were all deported from western Russia and forced to make new homes and lives for themselves in Siberia and Uzbekistan. For years, the Crimean Tatars did not have the right to return to their original homeland, although recently they have officially been permitted to do so. And it is not easy to find a Jew in any of the important departments of the Soviet administration.

For Khrushchev to have emphasized Stalin's treatment of nationalities would have been to admit that a form of racialism existed in the Soviet Union, and this would have meant linking official policy with one of the most abhorrent features of Nazi Germany.

In modern Russia, there has never been a single published law to impose special strictures on any particular people. Despite this handsome open-mindedness, certain more or less subtle official distinctions continue to exist. The nature of one's ethnic background must be indicated in one's passport, for instance.

The Question of Background

On reaching the age of sixteen, every Soviet citizen living in a town or industrial settlement is issued an identity card. This is an internal passport, valid only within the Soviet Union. On the first page of this document, immediately following the holder's name, address, and date of birth, comes a space for "nationality," which must be filled in with the nationality of the holder's parents. *Their* nationality is the determining factor. That space will show whether the owner of the passport is "Russian," "Kazakh," "Belorussian," "Jew," "Tatar," or whatever he may be.

If a person is born of a mixed marriage, the police give him the right to choose between the two nationalities shown in his parents' passports. This choice can be made only once in a lifetime, and, once set down, it is impossible to change it—even from your mother's to your father's—after the passport has been issued. A family counsel usually takes place in mixed families just before the choice has to be made, because everybody knows how important it is to have a "good" nationality. Where one of the parents is Russian, there is really nothing to take counsel about. It is obviously wise to choose "Russian" nationality, because that is the most privileged. But when both parents are non-Russians, the question is decided according to the value of their nationalities, and the special prejudices of the area in which they live. For example, in a mixed Tatar-Ukrainian family, the child will, as a rule, be registered as a Ukrainian, but in a Tatar-Jewish family as a Tatar. This is because it is better to be a Ukrainian than a Tatar, and better to be a Tatar than a Jew. In an Armenian-Georgian family living in the capital of Georgia, a son or daughter will choose to have Georgian nationality. But if the same family were living in Yerevan, the capital of Armenia, the children would be Armenians. And so forth.

The sixteen-year-old son of some friends of mine—a Russian father and a Jewish mother—told me with a bitter smile how surprised a police officer had been when he heard that the boy wanted to be registered as a Jew. The officer asked him, over and over again, what nationality the boy had decided to take, then made sure that this was being done with the agreement of all members of the family. Finally, he said with much emphasis, "Please bear in mind that your father is Russian and you therefore have *every right* to have Russian nationality entered in your passport." The official wanted to do the boy a good turn.

It is not, however, just a matter of passports. Whenever a Soviet citizen takes a new job or enters a university or even joins a sports club, whenever he moves, to go and live in a different town, and, of course, before he makes any journey abroad, he must fill in a questionnaire. These vary in the number and nature of the questions that must be answered. But every one of these official forms, regardless of its other questions, will certainly ask for your nationality. You are obliged to answer on the basis of what is noted in your passport. In any case, your answers are checked against your passport before your questionnaire is approved. And most questionnaires, incidentally, contain a warning of criminal responsibility should false answers be given.

Recently there have been rumors that the Central Committee of the Party had decided, quietly, to put an end to whatever bad feeling there may be between the various nationalities, and in particular to anti-Semitism. For this purpose, it was said, all Soviet citizens were to be provided with new passports that would contain no reference to nationality. Also, questions relating to this subject were to be removed from all official questionnaires.

I do not know the source of these rumors, though in Russia there is usually some trace of fact behind most political gossip. But it was only when I was to travel abroad, in 1966, that I carried a passport that made no mention of my "internal" nationality. And at that time, I was warned that when I came to fill out an immigration card on arrival in England, I was to write only "citizen of the U.S.S.R." in the place provided for "nationality." Nothing more.

To be a "Russian" in the Soviet Union is the equivalent of being a member of a somewhat privileged class. A member of almost any of the less preferred nationalities might be able to offer, with no great difficulty, examples of how he has been forced to suffer on occasion, because of the accident of his birth. Because I was born a Jew, the examples I can offer most readily have to do with what it means to be one of these in the Soviet Union.

The Jews

Two or three years ago, a French Communist visited the Soviet Union and carried out an interesting experiment. He announced that he had come to find out what the situation was with regard to the employment of Jews. He visited several factories, offices, and institutes, and everywhere he went he asked the man in charge the same question: How many Jews do you have working for you? Sometimes he would be given the figure at once, from memory. In other cases, the man in charge of the personnel deperatment would be summoned for the answer. But nowhere did the visitor have

to wait more than five minutes to be given an exact figure
for the number of Jews employed. Apparently this was true,
even when the question was asked at a large factory. At Moscow University, they not only told him the number of Jewish
students, but also told him what percentage they constituted
of the whole student body, adding with some pride that the
percentage was twice as high as it had been before the Revolution. It is not hard to draw some rather unpleasant infer-
ences from the immediacy of this kind of awareness of the
presence of a minority group.

Often enough, the number of Jews employed in a plant
or office may depend on where they happen to be situated.
Geography can often temper the tolerance with which the
Jew may be viewed by those around him. Thus, it is relatively easy for a Jew to find work in Georgia, and not especially difficult in Belorussia. But it is usually a considerable
problem for him to do so in the Ukraine. There, it would
seem, the old animus dies hard.

To be a Jew in the Soviet Union is, even today, something
that instills in those who bear the label a vague sense of
guilt. It conveys, at times in a way that is quite tangible, a
sense of one's being in some way inferior. It is for this reason
that many children of mixed marriages choose to be registered as "Russians." It also explains why many people change
their obviously Jewish names to more innocent Russian ones.
This will not alter the notation of background in one's passport, but it will permit the bearer to breathe a bit more easily
in public. Most Jewish writers and journalists in the Soviet
Union have chosen for this reason to work behind pseu-
donyms. I was one of them.

It is not possible for the Communist ideal to condone an
official anti-Semitic policy, but it is not possible, either, for
the notoriously sensitive leadership to permit any strong in-
group feelings that may threaten the ascendancy of the
official Party line. Any nationality group in the Soviet Union

that gave off too strong a political vibration would be more or less quietly hamstrung. In the case of the Jews, the emergence and survival of the state of Israel has provided a special degree of nervousness in the Kremlin. With perhaps 3 million Jews in Russia, there is always the possibility that the success of Israel, if not its very existence, will act like sunlight on a plant that has been long in the shadows. The plant may respond not necessarily to a sense of religious warmth, but rather to one of Jewish pride—for which one may read "nationalism." It may thus turn itself to face the warmth of that sun. And the sun of Israel, in these days of cosmic tension, shines from the West.

But in a way, with this problem, too, the hope of Russia is in her youth. The young people of the Soviet Union would seem to be totally devoid of anti-Jewish feeling. It will be recalled that Yevtushenko, who is not Jewish, created a sensation with his poem "Babi Yar," which shamed the government for its curious inhibitions about telling the whole story of the Nazi destruction of the Jewish community of Kiev. The young people of Russia have come to express themselves with more and more freedom on the subject of discrimination from above.

There is a superficial resemblance between the position of the Jew in the Soviet Union and that of the Negro in the United States. But I shall never forget the words I once heard from a non-Jewish Russian professor, a colonel in the air force: "Do you know the real difference between the position of our Jews and, say, the position of the Negroes in America? It is that the American Negroes have their own organizations and their own leaders and they fight openly for their rights, whereas in Russia the Jews don't fight and don't have any organizations, otherwise. . . . Anyway, the other differences are not really significant, my friend."

18

 A FEW LAST WORDS

It is difficult to explain how, as I lived my new life in London, I began to detect the inner distance between myself and all the other people around me. With a sense of unease, and at the same time with great curiosity, I recognized that in a very special way I was different from the Englishman, Indian, African, or any other of the national types among whom I lived. As a white man, there was nothing especially distinctive about me, and I saw and heard things just as other men did. But I *interpreted* what I saw and heard in a way that was unique. And that was the difference.

For example, I was embarrassed by the frankness with

which people talked about money. A British journalist asked an editor, in my presence, how much he was to be paid for an article. I was horrified. A dentist, having looked into my mouth and told me what needed to be done, said, "That will cost you three pounds." My immediate thought was, "Here's somebody making money out of medicine!" And when two little girls put a notice in the window of a house, reading "White mice for sale—twopence each," I was shocked that children were allowed to go into business.

At first I felt a sense of superiority over such people. I had never been involved in business, and never discussed money with my editors. I always took whatever they, in their wisdom, chose to give me.

When I lived in Russia I was often short of money, and I frequently would have liked to obtain more. But I never spoke about this openly, because it is just not done over there. The people around me were usually themselves short of money, many of them far worse off in this respect than I was. But although they might go around in worn-out socks or shoes, they would never, for instance, ask for a raise in salary at their jobs. And in Russia, you just don't say, "I would like to have such and such a job, because it pays more." In the first place, you would probably not get the job. In the second, you would get the reputation of being a man who worked only for the sake of money. If you want to be given a job that appeals to you, the approved procedure is more like this: You are attracted to that particular job because you have a special vocation or facility for doing it well, and it is therefore the kind of work that will help you bring the greatest benefit to your country.

Yet, in practice, almost everyone in Russia today works for the sake of money. Highly paid positions become the object of "politics," intrigue, and downright scheming. But there are no references to that crassly capitalistic word "money."

On one occasion, I happened to be passing the entrance of

a luxurious nightclub in Mayfair. I watched the top-hatted doorman helping wealthy men and women to alight from their splendid limousines, and I had an instinctive feeling of resentment toward them. My thoughts went something like this: Freedom is all very well, but it doesn't make capitalism a good thing. In one evening, these people are going to squander enough money to support a working-class family for a month.

I had these thoughts even though I knew that the contrast between rich and poor in Russia is as great as in most capitalist countries. I also knew that the average working-class family in Britain has enough to eat, is adequately clothed, and is able to live in—luxury of luxuries!—its own *private* flat. And often it lives even in its own house.

But I reacted as I did because in Russia the highly privileged usually conceal themselves behind the fences of their villas and find their amusements among their own friends. As a rule they are hidden from view, too, by barriers put up by the secret and the not-so-secret police. Capitalist inequality is visible, I kept noticing, while the Communist kind tends to be out of obvious view, as if it were carefully stored somewhere in an official closet. Those fortunate Soviet citizens who have managed to accumulate wealth—such as some writers and composers, for example—usually throw a veil over their affluence, for fear that they may be considered "capitalists."

I was able to notice another difference between me and those about me who were not Russian, but this had more to do with Freud. Sitting opposite me in the London underground, a young couple would turn to each other from time to time and kiss. I would try not to watch them, thinking, "They should be ashamed of themselves!" My reaction was the standard one of a Soviet citizen. Such behavior is considered extremely improper there, as is, indeed, any direct reference to sex. Russia is a country of considerable sexual activity, not all of it entirely moral by conventional standards. Marital infidelity is hardly uncommon, and the life of the flesh is pursued there with a kind of candor that would be considered striking in quite a few countries of the West. But even a dedicated philanderer, there, would never kiss his companion on a train in the Moscow subway, for instance, not even if he were quite drunk. Bred in the bone of every modern Russian is the knowledge that his interest in this, like his need for money, is not a matter for public display.

As I tried to analyze my reactions in London, I checked them with those of compatriots who had left Russia recently. I discovered that they, too, had had many of these same disquieting feelings. This led me to some rather gloomy conclusions. Here I was, a man with a pretty good idea of the nature of the Soviet system, who had even been through the prison camps, and who had fled from the country, and yet I was still saturated with Soviet attitudes and ways of thinking. If this was true of me, then what was there to be said about the millions living in Russia who took the system for granted?

My London reactions were personal, even trivial perhaps, but they set me to do some additional thinking about the country I had left.

The Drift of Russia

Scientists maintain that the continents are not fixed inexorably in their places, but are actually moving. Although this drift is too slow to be observed, it is always going on. And in the social and political sense, Russia is like a drifting continent. You will not see any substantial or clearly defined movement in any particular direction, and there are even those who believe that "the Revolution has come to a halt." But it will help us to understand what is going on in Russia if we talk not about movement, but about drift.

Sailors on a drifting ship never know where they will be on

the next day. People living in my country have this same problem about what to expect from each tomorrow. It may bring a rise or fall in prices and another 180-degree turn in relations with China. A period of fierce ideological pressure will be followed by one of comparative relaxation, and then it may be discovered that that relaxation was a "mistake on the part of the previous leaders." Rumors abound, now to encourage and now to dismay. People will be exhorted to use only public transport, and there will be concurrent attacks on those who own their own cars. Along with this, there will be talk of increasing the output of cars for private use. One day de Gaulle is down, the next day up. Mao Tsetung, vice versa. The list of "movements," "initiatives," and "campaigns" that have died and been forgotten almost before launching is very long.

The most extraordinary reading in Russia is that provided by copies of old newspapers—those, say, of a year ago. They contain names that it is today forbidden to mention. They discuss a "movement to transfer the machines in the factories to the safekeeping of the workers," which has since been denounced as bureaucratic nonsense. Every other paragraph contains a reference to the "twenty-year plan," about which it has long been forbidden to talk. And so forth.

This is what I mean by drift. There is a lack of clearly defined direction. But if you study the path of a drifting ship, it is always possible to discern a somewhat general direction of movement. This is also true, I believe, of the Soviet Union.

Many Russians have the feeling that the central power of the country is becoming steadily less obvious, if not weaker. There are orders issued from the Kremlin today that are regarded with less urgency, at the action level, than they were in the days when someone's head might roll for lack of instant compliance. Another sign is in the new attitude toward former holy places like *Pravda*. In the old days, a critical article there, dealing with the work of a factory manager, would have meant the end of him. Today, things are different. People are no longer in such a hurry to demand summary judgment for a man who has been officially attacked. The influence of the press has declined greatly. Readers even draw attention now to "inaccuracies" that have appeared in the newspapers. A kind of erosion of authority seems to have set in, in a number of areas.

Communism began as an orthodoxy zealously pursued by a few believers, each of its dogmas clutched fiercely to the breast. But like all orthodoxies that have achieved power —the Catholic Church is one other example—it has been forced to modify its tenets to meet the challenge of major responsibility, of survival, of facing matters that are known on the humbler, personal level as "reality." For a great many years, the Soviet Union was operated in the manner of a "company town." Nothing was permitted that was considered detrimental to the interests of those who in effect "owned" everything in sight. And the Russian landlords also owned the lives of the inhabitants.

By now, Soviet ideology, battered by necessity, has begun to show the results of this wear and tear. This fact is admitted in the Central Committee itself. Many discussions have been held there about the need for "more attractive presentation" of the official point of view, and for a "more effective propaganda." But the old unthinking zeal, the relentless dedication to dogma, has declined.

People now breathe more easily about those who are in power. Even a high Party official can no longer liquidate a subordinate on the basis of mere personal whim.

And then there are the young people of Russia. Many of them have little faith in propaganda and little experience of the terrible personal dread that suffused the Soviet past. They are not so easily led to follow orders blindly, but are likely at times to demand explanations.

I hasten to point out that a large number of people in Russia are not pleased with this weakening of central authority. Forget the out-and-out Stalinists, who continue to sigh for the "good old days." I am speaking of the middle and older generations, who have grown so accustomed to the yoke that they now feel uncomfortable and worried without it. There are people at all levels of the regime, from the topmost committee down to the factory workshop, who regret the change. The fact that they have to make decisions, even relatively minor ones, is very troubling for them.

In the old days, it was the boss giving the order who bore the responsibility. He, in his turn, received his instructions ready-made from above. As long as he transmitted the order to those beneath him, he was fulfilling his duty. A person accustomed throughout his life to that kind of passive role may be easily confused under today's newer ground rules. The immediate boss today does not get his conveniently packaged instructions handed to him from above. When his subordinates bring questions to him, he may try to thrust the responsibility right back onto their shoulders: "Just make up your own mind," he may say, adding that "Things are different now." Those below him may now have their share of his new problems.

In an odd way, a basic principle of Communism has been applied to the decision-making process—it has been nationalized. Its rewards—and responsibilities—have been allocated over a wider, more democratic area, and not all recipients are grateful for the gift.

Nevertheless, those who are sighing for a strong hand are in the minority. The greater part of the population, especially those under forty, have been happy to bid good riddance to it. People have begun to think more readily for themselves, despite the systematic hammerings of the propaganda barrage, and the sense of "the collective" so carefully instilled by the educational apparatus.

The atmosphere has changed, become somewhat freed from the rigid constraints of the past. Many Russians are becoming increasingly aware of the discrepancy between the political, social, and economic claims of the regime, and the realities. And they are speaking more openly about the shortcomings of the Soviet system. But the system remains largely unchanged. The post-Stalin improvements have been more a relaxation of certain aspects of the regime than any change in its basic structure or even policy.

If we generalize about the ordinary people of Russia, it must be said that they have no clearly defined yearning for political liberties. They have had very little experience with democratic institutions so familiar to the West. For too many of them, the old tight-fitting cloak of official repression is one they are used to. It does not serve them, in their minds, as quite the Iron Maiden it is conceived to be in freer countries. A person who has never seen an oyster is scarcely eager to eat it when he comes upon it for the first time. And it is hard to explain the beauty of a summer sky to a man who has been blind from birth. These days I am often asked, because I am a Russian, "What is going to happen over there?" But even the captain of a ship adrift can only guess the ultimate direction of the aimless course. As one of the crew who jumped ship some time ago, I, too, have certain problems about viewing its future. But guessing at political trends is a universal form of self-indulgence, and I am not immune to it.

My own experience leads me to believe that very few Russians are interested in bringing about the kind of regime that could be labeled "capitalist." They would probably be quite happy, rather, with a more moderate form of the kind of planned economy that they now have.

It is a fact of history that industrialism produces changes not only in the life of the state but in that of the average man as well. And such changes (individual well-being, blunted orthodoxies, the rise of special interest groups, to name a few) are bound to influence the shape of the Russia that lurks beyond the horizon of the coming years.

The proliferation of good housing and of decent and plentiful consumer goods may give greater impetus to the motivations of the average citizen that have in the past been denounced as "bourgeois" or "individualistic." This, in any case, is the opinion of more experienced analysts of world affairs than myself.

I tend to believe, with others, that the present one-party system in Russia has entered a period of decline. How long this period will last, I cannot even speculate, but in time, I feel, it will give way to a more flexible—or less inflexible—system. Perhaps it will be transformed along the lines of the Yugoslav model. No cataclysm from outside or inside the Soviet Union is required to produce this result. All that is necessary is that the freer, less rigid rhythms that have been set in motion in recent years be permitted to evolve. And I can see no way that these can be slowed down or stopped. Russia's drift would seem to be toward a measure of freedom. But no matter how much I will it for my fellow Russians, how soon freedom will come—and how much of it will come—I cannot say.

INDEX